Legacy
Leadership

*Principles for Leaving
a Spiritual Legacy*

M. Reid Ward

Legacy Leadership: Principles for Leaving a Spiritual Legacy
© Copyright 2008 Michael Reid Ward
Published by:
        Legacy Leadership Ministry, Inc.
        PO Box 796
        Troy, Alabama 36081
        (334) 268-2503
        www.legacyleadershipministry.org

ISBN: 1-4196-9644-0
EAN-13: 978-1-4196-9644-2
First Printing

All rights reserved. No part of this work may be reproduced, stored in a retrieval system, or transmitted in any form or by any means, electronic or mechanical, including photocopying and recording, without express written permission of the publisher. Requests for permission should be addressed to Legacy Ministries, PO Box 796, Troy, Alabama 36081

Unless otherwise indicated, all Scripture quotations are taken from the New American Standard Bible
Copyright © 1960, 1962, 1968, 1971, 1972, 1973, 1975, 1977, 1995 by The Lockman Foundation. Used by permission.

To purchase additional copies of this resource:
BookSurge Publishing
www.booksurge.com
orders@booksurge.com
1-866-308-6235

Printed by: BookSurge Publishing
                Charleston, South Carolina

Cover design by: Jodi Rankin Daniels
                     Pharmgurhl Graphics

Dedication

To my wife, Rayanne, who has
been loving, loyal, and the
greatest example of these
principles in my life.

To Jimmy Ward and Jody Rankin:
I can not imagine two
men I would rather my
children have as grandfathers.

To my children, Trinity Grace, Elijah Andrew,
and Zachariah Steven, who are the light of my soul,
the primary focus of my life, and the
true measure of my legacy.

Enter His gates with thanksgiving
And His courts with praise.
Give thanks to Him, bless His name.
For the LORD is good;
His loving kindness is everlasting
And His faithfulness to all generations.
PSALM 100:4-5

Special Thanks to:

Jerry Deloney, for years of faithful service on the Legacy Board of Directors.

The Legacy Ministries Board of Directors for their unending support.

Randy Bruner, my partner in founding Legacy Ministries for half of the ideas in this book.

Erin Warde, my proof reader.

Mitchell Harris, for mentoring these thoughts.
Dr. John Brennan, for challenging me to write.
Drew, Matt, John, Shelly and Kristal from Sandersville, GA for first confirming the call.

Bush Memorial Baptist Church, Rangeline Baptist Church, Faunsdale Presbyterian Church, and Elk Creek Baptist Church.

Dr. Tom Nettles, John & Emma Hicks, the Parrott Family, Scott Dawson, Four Days Late, and Dale Glover.

I love you Mom!

CONTENTS

INTRODUCTION vii

INFLUENCE 1
Chapter 1 Setting a Standard of Excellence:
           Being What God Created and Called You to Be 7

Chapter 2 Influence:
           A Mandate to Lead 21

IMPACT 37
Chapter 3 Integrity:
           Character Determines Impact 41

Chapter 4 Integrity:
           Five Biblical Relationships 51

Chapter 5 Insight:
           Seeing God's Will 65

Chapter 6 Imitation:
           Walking in Christ 75

Chapter 7 Intensity:
           Counting the Costs 87

LEGACY 101
Chapter 8 Purpose:
           Why We Lead 107

Chapter 9 Moses:
           A Legacy Leadership Model 125

INTRODUCTION

Everywhere you look these days there is a book about leadership. People are reading about it, talking about it and thinking about it all of the time. Leadership has always been important in every area of life. However, I think one of the reasons that leadership seems particularly important in our day and time is because there seems to be such a lack of it.

One look at our culture and you become aware that we are in a leadership crisis. In almost every institution in our country there is a void of authentic leadership. Our government is full of people who are clouded by selfish motivation and controlled by opinion polls. Corporate America is littered with examples of leadership that lacks integrity and courage. Our churches, unfortunately, are lead largely by men, people who are blown by every wind of culture and who are marked by reactionary methodology instead of biblical leadership. Our homes, most tellingly, are simply un-lead. We have lost entire generations because of the lack of true spiritual leadership in the home.

Though we are spending more time and money on leadership than ever before, it seems we have fewer and fewer real leaders. In fact, the leadership generation seems to be characterized by a lack of authentic leaders. Our leaders seem to be more like thermometers than thermostats. They are more blown by every wind of mass production and mass media than being pillars of strength, standing firm in the face of any and all storms.

I believe that is because the leadership generation is also the generation of identity management. It seems we have more time for Facebook and Myspace than we do for introspection and reflection. We spend more time managing what other people think about us than we do on who we really are. Our leaders spend more time doing research and reading opinion polls than they do searching for truth, standing by principle, and living by conviction. For the most part, we are not lead by any of the latter or by people who think much of them. Instead, we are lead in much the same way as we live.

It would be easy to say that this was all simply the product of our self-centered, entertainment-driven culture. While in large part it may be, in our rush to be relevant in our culture, our spiritual leaders have taken on much of the same quick-fix, leadership-is-influence mentality. Many spiritual leaders simply try to satisfy the greatest number of people for the largest majority of time in order to get all of the things that they desire from them. The principle reason that only ten percent of people who profess to be Christians have an authentic worldview is because ninety percent of Christians share the largely humanist worldviews of their leaders.

What we need in the midst of this leadership-drenched-yet-leaderless culture is real biblical leadership. There is no claim here on my part to have achieved any form of perfection. In fact, the heart of this book reflects Paul's sentiment when he says in Philippians 3:12–15, *"Not that I have already obtained this or am already perfect, but I press on to make it my own, because Christ Jesus has made me his own. Brothers, I do not consider that I have made it my own. But one thing I do: forgetting what lies behind and straining forward to what lies ahead, I press on toward the goal for the prize of the upward call of God in Christ Jesus. Let those of us who are mature think this way, and if in anything you think otherwise, God will reveal that also to you."*

However, I believe that God has called us all to be leaders, to be examples of what a believer should look like. As a result, I think what we need are spiritual leaders who are not trying to use their influence to get things done (or just to get things), but spiritual leaders who are willing to say with Paul, "follow me as I follow Christ." We need leaders who are willing to live the life of love, by giving up their lives sacrificially to walk in a manner worthy of their calling, to walk in love, patience, gentleness, and unity. We need leaders who are willing to take up their cross and follow to death, to stand firm at home, at church, at work, and at school.

God has called us all to use our influence for His kingdom, and not just use our influence, but to use it in a way that makes a lasting impact in peoples lives, an impact that is generational and leaves a legacy. He has given us clear principles for living that kind of life in His revelation of His own nature and character, the Bible.

This book is the fruit of teaching leadership over the past several years. My intention is to bring some of those messages together in a way that communicates what God expects out of us as spiritual leaders in the home, in the church and in the community. The idea is simple. We have true spiritual influence in the lives of the people around us when we make Christ the only standard of excellence in our lives and we answer the call of God to be examples of what a believer should look like. However, that influence may be short-lived and only has a lasting impact when people see us moving from where we are to where God wants us to be.

That maturing process is marked by several characteristics. First, we must have integrity in our lives and in our relationships to others. Second, we must demonstrate insight into the purpose and plan of God. Third, our walk must be characterized by the nature and character of Christ as we give ourselves to being imitators of Christ. Finally, that walk should have an intensity to it that reflects the reality that we are engaged in a spiritual warfare of epic and eternal proportions.

When our leadership takes on that quality and character, we are ready to lead generationally. That means that our influence will not only have impact, but it will leave a legacy of faithfulness long after we are gone. This is the model of leadership throughout Scripture and the natural result of our becoming what God created and called us to be.

INFLUENCE

Patrick Henry (1736–1799) was a member of the Virginia House of Burgesses and the Continental Congress. He was a leader in the Virginia Militia and was governor of Virginia (1776–1779, 1784). Henry was one of the colonies' foremost patriots in the growing revolutionary cause. As a fierce opponent of the Stamp Act, some say his Stamp Act Resolutions were the first shot fired in the Revolutionary War. Have you ever heard someone speak so passionately and with such conviction that the speech moved you to do something? Patrick Henry had that kind of influence in the American colonies.

He was a natural leader and a brilliant speaker; however, he is remembered mainly for the speech he gave to the Second Virginia Convention on March 23, 1775. The convention's task was to decide whether to arm the Virginia militia to fight the British. Henry's vision, faith, intensity, sense of calling and purpose had a great influence on the members of that congress and those residing throughout the colonies. As the fate of liberty hung in the balance, the influence of one man helped to change the course of history.[1]

---

[1] Patrick Henry, Independence Hall Association, Philadelphia, Pennsylvania. Published electronically at www.ushistory.org. On the Internet since July 4, 1995. 1999-2005.

Give Me Liberty or Give Me Death

No man thinks more highly than I do of the patriotism, as well as abilities, of the very worthy gentlemen who have just addressed the House. But different men often see the same subject in different lights; and, therefore, I hope it will not be thought disrespectful to those gentlemen if, entertaining as I do opinions of a character very opposite to theirs, I shall speak forth my sentiments freely and without reserve. This is no time for ceremony. The question before the House is one of awful moment to this country. For my own part, I consider it as nothing less than a question of freedom or slavery; and in proportion to the magnitude of the subject ought to be the freedom of the debate. It is only in this way that we can hope to arrive at truth, and fulfill the great responsibility which we hold to God and our country. Should I keep back my opinions at such a time, through fear of giving offense, I should consider myself as guilty of treason towards my country, and of an act of disloyalty toward the Majesty of Heaven, which I revere above all earthly kings.

Mr. President, it is natural to man to indulge in the illusions of hope. We are apt to shut our eyes against a painful truth, and listen to the song of that siren till she transforms us into beasts. Is this the part of wise men, engaged in a great and arduous struggle for liberty? Are we disposed to be of the number of those who, having eyes, see not, and, having ears, hear not, the things which so nearly concern their temporal salvation? For my part, whatever anguish of spirit it may cost, I am willing to know the whole truth; to know the worst, and to provide for it.

I have but one lamp by which my feet are guided, and that is the lamp of experience. I know of no way of judging of the future but by the past. And judging by the past, I wish to know what there has been in the conduct of the British ministry for the last ten years to justify those hopes with which gentlemen have been pleased to solace themselves and the House. Is it that insidious smile with which our petition has been lately received? Trust it not, sir; it will prove a snare to your feet. Suffer not yourselves to be betrayed with a kiss. Ask yourselves how this gracious reception of our petition comports with those warlike preparations which cover our waters and darken our land. Are fleets and armies necessary to a work of love and reconciliation? Have we shown ourselves so unwilling to be reconciled that force must be called in to win back our love?

Let us not deceive ourselves, sir. These are the implements of war and subjugation; the last arguments to which kings resort. I ask gentlemen, sir, what means this martial array, if its purpose be not to force us to submission? Can gentlemen assign any other possible motive for it? Has Great Britain any enemy, in this quarter of the world, to call for all this accumulation of navies and armies? No, sir, she has none. They are meant for us: they can be meant for no other. They are sent over to bind and rivet upon us those chains which the British ministry have been so long forging. And what have we to oppose to them? Shall we try argument? Sir, we have been trying that for the last ten years. Have we anything new to offer upon the subject? Nothing. We have held the subject up in every light of which it is capable; but it has been all in vain. Shall we resort to entreaty and humble supplication? What terms shall we find which have not been already exhausted?

Let us not, I beseech you, sir, deceive ourselves. Sir, we have done everything that could be done to avert the storm which is now coming on. We have petitioned; we have remonstrated; we have supplicated; we have prostrated ourselves before the throne, and have implored its interposition to arrest the tyrannical hands of the ministry and Parliament. Our petitions have been slighted; our remonstrance's have produced additional violence and insult; our supplications have been disregarded; and we have been spurned, with contempt, from the foot of the throne! In vain, after these things, may we indulge the fond hope of peace and reconciliation. There is no longer any room for hope. If we wish to be free—if we mean to preserve inviolate those inestimable privileges for which we have been so long contending—if we mean not basely to abandon the noble struggle in which we have been so long engaged, and which we have pledged ourselves never to abandon until the glorious object of our contest shall be obtained—we must fight! I repeat it, sir, we must fight! An appeal to arms and to the God of hosts is all that is left us!

They tell us, sir, that we are weak; unable to cope with so formidable an adversary. But when shall we be stronger? Will it be the next week, or the next year? Will it be when we are totally disarmed, and when a British guard shall be stationed in every house? Shall we gather strength by irresolution and inaction? Shall we acquire the means of effectual resistance by lying supinely on our backs and hugging the delusive phantom of hope, until our enemies shall have bound us hand and foot? Sir, we are not weak if we make a proper use of those means which the God of nature hath placed in our power. The millions of people, armed in the holy cause of liberty, and in such a country as that which we possess, are invincible by any force which our enemy can send against us. Besides, sir, we shall not fight our battles alone. There is a just God who presides over the destinies of nations, and who will raise up friends to fight our battles for us. The battle, sir, is not to the strong alone; it is to the vigilant, the active, the brave. Besides, sir, we have no election. If we were base enough to desire it, it is now too late to retire from the contest. There is no retreat but in submission and slavery! Our chains are forged! Their clanking may be heard on the plains of Boston! The war is inevitable--and let it come! I repeat it, sir, let it come.

It is in vain, sir, to extenuate the matter. Gentlemen may cry, Peace, Peace—but there is no peace. The war is actually begun! The next gale that sweeps from the north will bring to our ears the clash of resounding arms! Our brethren are already in the field! Why stand we here idle? What is it that gentlemen wish? What would they have? Is life so dear, or peace so sweet, as to be purchased at the price of chains and slavery? Forbid it, Almighty God! I know not what course others may take; but as for me, give me liberty or give me death!

CHAPTER 1

SETTING A STANDARD OF EXCELLENCE:
Being what God created and called you to be

For me to live is Christ and to die is gain.
PHILIPPIANS 1:21

> Every soul he [Paul] came in contact with was an opportunity; and all his life, so far as active service went, was poured out in the doing of this one thing: the bringing of men who had never seen the Christ into a place where they might see Him; and the building up of those who had seen Him in their most holy faith from height to height, and from glory unto glory. The whole aim and influence of his life was Christ.
> G. Campbell Morgan
> *The True Estimate of Life*

We all have a standard in life to which we measure ourselves or which serves as a goal to us, often with it being the person next to us. It is a natural thing in life to measure ourselves against other people. We want to see how we are doing by looking at the lives of others and evaluating our progress as compared to theirs. It is comforting to see people who struggle just as we do and inspiring to see others who have persevered or achieved great things in life. Those other people in our lives serve as a measuring stick that we use to gauge, encourage, and motivate ourselves.

We can also use other people as a source of excuse or discouragement. We view them as a measuring stick in our lives to which we can never measure up and therefore as an excuse to never try and reach our potential. That is part of what is powerful about peer pressure. It is the idea that we in turn are measured by the people around us, and we are affected by what they think of us. So, we follow the crowd, and do what our peers do. More importantly, we measure ourselves by their standard. Though that can have a positive impact on our lives, it more often has a negative effect.

The standard that we have established in our lives may be our parents. That's right! As much as it is common to deny the influence of our parents, we have to admit that they often serve as a standard in our lives. Many of us grow up watching our parents and learning much of what we know from them. We measure our development as people against the example they set for us. Everything that I knew in my early life about love, work, sacrifice, and fun I learned from my parents. Our faith should be, and often is, founded and nurtured by the example and influence of our parents. They can serve as the most positive and influential measuring stick and most of us do not realize how much that is true until we are well into our adult lives.

For some, parents serve as a negative example. For far too many people today, parents are the source of a lot of their trouble. However, we remain under their influence, and must work very hard to understand how to be set free from the cycle of life into which we have been brought. Often, parents set bad examples in relationships, work ethic, and faith. Though we are clearly called by God to be obedient to them as the authority over us, we must also discern how to hold true to the conscience that works in us by the Holy Spirit.

Perhaps the hardest thing to deal with is the expectations of our parents. It does not matter if the expectations are clearly expressed or simply communicated in their values and way of life, these expectations can be a weight that proves too heavy to bear. If we allow ourselves to be measured by the expectations of others, including our parents, we are choosing to live in bondage. In Christ's work on the cross, we were set free to be who God created and called us to be. We have a liberty and freedom in Christ from all of the expectations of what other people want us to be. Far too often we allow the expectations of others to define us and tell us what we are here for and who we are supposed to be.

Some of us may have established a historical figure or cultural icon as a standard in our lives. When I was growing up, athletes served as major standards in my life. Like most little boys, I remember dreaming of being Danny White, Walter Peyton, Larry Bird, or maybe even Magic Johnson or John Riggins. However, it was Michael Jordan who became a real standard in my life. It was an unrealistic standard. I am aware of that. However, it was very real to me. I wanted to be like Mike in every way. Basketball had long been my favorite sport and the object of most of my dreams. But by the time I was in middle school, my obsession with being the best basketball player around, as well as the "be like Mike" mantra, was full blown. I memorized every story of his childhood and basketball career. I worked very hard to be great, and my standard of greatness was #23 for the Chicago Bulls.

Now, not all of them may be that obvious and obsessive, but most of us have some historical or cultural figure that we look up to as a picture of who we would like to be. It was a seemingly harmless infatuation for me until I graduated from high school. In fact, my quest taught me many valuable lessons, and athletics served to make me a stronger and more confident person. I learned the value of a team and the importance of hard work, setting goals and striving to achieve. However, when I graduated from high school, my dream began to shatter and two things became overwhelmingly obvious. First, my identity as a person was so closely tied to being a basketball player that when that no longer defined who I was,

I suffered a huge identity crisis. Second, basketball had been so important to me that it had taken the place of God. Although the goal of being like Mike had many positive effects, setting his life and success up as a standard proved to be a foolishly disastrous endeavor.

In our postmodern context, the standard that we set up as a measuring stick may even be ourselves. Far from evaluating ourselves honestly, we often make ourselves the gold standard. Whatever we think is good or right is going to be how we measure the value of our life and actions. Contemporary thought does not acknowledge absolute truth, and therefore whatever is true for you in your context or in a certain circumstance must be true.

If we set our own conscience and convictions up as the standard, we must be mindful how easily we can be manipulated by our own emotions. If our conscience is not guided by the Holy Spirit and the truth of God's word, it will be led around by the deceitful desires of the flesh, which leads to destruction. The entire basis of Christianity is that there is absolute truth that flows out of the reality of the nature and character of God and that truth is revealed in the actual words of Scripture. This assures us that there is a standard of what is right that exists outside of ourselves.

What is a Standard?

The problem with using any of these examples as a standard is that they are not perfect. They are either internal or changing. For a standard to be true, it must be external and eternal. In Sevres, France, there is a place called the International Bureau of Weights and Measures (BIPM). The task of the BIPM is to ensure the worldwide uniformity of measurements and their traceability to the International System of Units. In 1889, the Convention of the Meter was convened by fifty-one nations to form a treaty on the accurate measure of a meter, and the BIPM was formed to keep up with the most up-to-date and scientific standards of measurement in the world.

The 1889 definition of a meter was based on the international prototype of platinum-iridium. It was replaced in 1960 by a definition using the wavelength of krypton 86 radiation. In 1983, this definition replaced it: "The meter is the length of the path traveled by light in a vacuum during a time interval of 1/299,792,458 of a second." Time has a similar standard definition. "The second is the duration of 9,192,631,770 periods of the radiation corresponding to the transition between the two hyperfine levels of the ground state of the caesium 133 atom." However, it seems weight, the kilogram in particular, is the base standard for all measurements. Its definition reads like this, "The kilogram is the unit of mass; it is equal to the mass of the international prototype of the kilogram." What is the point in all of this? In France there is a place where they keep all of the measurement standards of the physical world, and science recognizes that there has to be such a thing as absolutes—an external and eternal standard by which to measure things.

The Bible tells us that the same thing is true for us spiritually and as human beings. We are to have ultimately only one standard in our lives. There is only one standard for all humanity that is external and eternal, that serves as a true and original measure. That standard is Christ Jesus. Philippians tells us that Christ is the only perfect standard, and that we should have our eyes fixed on Him alone as the measuring stick.

> *Let us therefore, as many as are perfect, have this attitude; and if in anything you have a different attitude, God will reveal that also to you; however, let us keep living by that same standard to which we have attained. Brethren, join in following my example, and observe those who walk according to the pattern you have in us.* PHILIPPIANS 3:15–17

The life of Christ serves as a standard for which we are to strive, establishing it as the goal and reflecting to others as an example that they can follow in becoming what God created and called them to be.

Establishing a Standard

How do we establish the standard of Christ in our lives? The first thing that we have to understand is that Christ as the standard implies that we will no longer allow ourselves to be defined by the opinions and expectations of others. We will not be measured by houses, lands, popularity or social status. We must set our minds on the fact that we are ultimately not measured by the things of this world, but by God, and that God will measure by the standard of Christ.

The second thing that we have to understand is that we cannot fully attain the standard of Christ on our own. He was virgin born, He lived completely without sin, and His standard is one of complete righteousness. That is to say that He is completely right in everything that He says or does. He is the standard of what is right, and because we are weak and sinful in our nature, we cannot attain righteousness on our own. We need His help.

The third thing that we have to understand is that we have to be transformed by receiving the fruit of righteousness, which comes through Jesus.

> *And this I pray, that your love may abound still more and more in real knowledge and all discernment, so that you may approve the things that are excellent, in order to be sincere and blameless until the day of Christ; having been filled with the fruit of righteousness which comes through Jesus Christ, to the glory and praise of God.* PHILIPPIANS 1:9–11

When Christ took our place on the cross in order to pay the debt of sin for us, He took on our sin, and by receiving what Christ did on the cross, we receive His righteousness. Not only this, but through our adoption as children of God, we receive the inheritance of heaven and the seal of that promise, the Holy Spirit. It is by receiving Christ's righteousness and living under the control of the Holy Spirit that we are transformed and made able to live by that same standard of rightness that we have attained through Christ. Even by the power of the Spirit, we are unable to live up to the standard of Christ perfectly until we know as we are known in eternity. However, by that power we are able to grow in spiritual maturity, from height unto height and glory unto glory, even unto the likeness of Christ.

Reflecting the Standard

Not only are we to establish Christ as the standard by receiving His righteousness and following Him by the power of the Holy Spirit, but we are to also reflect or be an example of the standard of Christ to others. How can we be an example of such a high standard? How can we say with Paul, "Follow me as I follow Christ"? First, we have to be transformed, as Romans 12 tells us, by the renewing of our minds. We must be transformed in our thinking.

> *Finally, brethren, whatever is true, whatever is honorable, whatever is right, whatever is pure, whatever is lovely, whatever is of good repute, if there is any excellence and if anything worthy of praise, dwell on these things.* PHILIPPIANS 4:8

In order for us to reflect Christ in our lives, we have to change the way we think. Philippians 4:8 tells us that we have to dwell on the things of God. For much of our lives, we are bombarded with sights and sounds that cause us to dwell on the things of the world. We listen to music or watch television and movies, and we do not realize that we are putting worldly information into our heads. The result is that when we are in our idle thoughts or when our world grows quiet, we are still hearing and seeing things that are not true, honorable, lovely and right. This is a major problem for us when it hampers our ability to hear God and dwell on the things of God.

Test for yourself. When you go to bed at night and you are staring up at the ceiling in the darkness, what thoughts and images are going through your mind? What sounds of the day are ringing in your ears? Is it the sounds of the world, or is it the still, small voice of God? The Bible does not tell us not to watch television or movies. It does not tell us to what music to listen. The Bible tells us to be careful what you hear and see, to understand where it comes from, and to dwell on the things that are excellent and worthy of praise.

Second, we have to be transformed in our attitude. We know from the verse we read earlier in Philippians 3 that there is a particular attitude that we are to have. In reference to attaining the resurrection from the dead and spiritual maturity, Paul describes the attitude that he means.

> *Not that I have already obtained it or have already become perfect, but I press on so that I may lay hold of that for which also I was laid hold of by Christ Jesus. Brethren, I do not regard myself as having laid hold of it yet; but one thing I do: forgetting what lies behind and reaching forward to what lies ahead, I press on toward the goal for the prize of the upward call of God in Christ Jesus.* PHILIPPIANS 3:12–14

This attitude of pressing forward grows out of an understanding of what Christ has done for us. Paul uses the analogy of a runner to describe the Christian's spiritual growth. He understands that he has not reached his goal of Christ-likeness. The thing here to be obtained is the resurrection from the dead, but that resurrection comes through the process of knowing Christ, knowing His power, sharing in His sufferings, and becoming like Him in submission to God or like Him in His death.

Paul says he is not there yet, just as none of us are quite there yet, nor is he already perfect. Now this perfection is not the idea of being without fault, but it is the idea of completion, or in this case, spiritual maturity. He says, "I am still a work in progress, a work that has been completed for me, but not yet completed in me."

Paul also acknowledges that he has not yet taken possession of the prize for which he runs. He makes it clear that he is running for a prize, a particular prize: eternal fellowship with God through the work of Christ and the process of sanctification. However, he does not consider that he has made that prize his own. Again, he has been taken hold of for the purpose of receiving this prize, but he has not yet taken hold of it or made it his own. However, he presses on to take hold of the prize—to take hold of the eternal life to which he was called. We press on to make it our own, to lay hold of that for which Christ laid hold of us. Because knowing Christ and being found in Him is the greatest possible gift, the greatest good news. Christ chose Paul for the ultimate purpose of conforming Paul to His glorious image (Romans 8:29), and that is the very goal Paul pursued to attain. This "pressing on" attitude should cause us to live life with an attitude that has a different character to it because of the great value of the prize.

> *Do everything without complaining or arguing, so that*
> *you may become blameless and pure, children of God*
> *without fault in a crooked and depraved generation,*

> *in which you shine like stars in the universe as you hold out the word of life—in order that I may boast on the day of Christ that I did not run or labor for nothing.* PHILIPPIANS 2:14–16 (NIV)

The goal is that we become what God created and called us to be, "blameless and pure." Again, we understand that this is something that we cannot do by our own power. We do this by living without complaining or arguing. This is a great challenge to us in a time when everyone thinks in terms of personal rights and entitlements. We have to truly be transformed in our thinking and understand as Paul did that to live is Christ.

This is such a key concept because our transformation into the image of Christ requires our submission to God and our humility before others. We complain because we are not getting what we think we deserve or something we think we ought to get, or because things are not going the way we want them to or the way we think they ought. The source of that kind of attitude is pride, and it reveals a lack of faith in the good, pleasing, and perfect will of God. We argue because we believe we are right. We all believe we are right. If we did not, we would think a different way. No one thinks he is wrong and goes on thinking in the same way. We all think we are right, and we argue because we want other people to know we are right and to acknowledge it, thus acknowledging that they are wrong. We argue because we are proud and we want others to submit to us, when we should be submitting to God. We do not have to get run over or be taken advantage of to be able to give an account of what we believe efficiently and passionately. We should always be prepared to defend the truth of God's word. However, we must not be complainers or arguers. We are to be like shining stars in the universe, light and salt in a dark and tasteless world.

Finally, we have to be transformed in our conduct. To reflect a standard to the world, they must be able to see it in us. We must be transformed in our thoughts and attitudes in order for the standard to be a reality in us, but we must be transformed in our speech and conduct in order for others to see the standard reflected in us.

> *Only conduct yourselves in a manner worthy of the gospel of Christ, so that whether I come and see you or remain absent, I will hear of you that you are standing firm in one spirit, with one mind striving together for the faith of the gospel;* PHILIPPIANS 1:27

In Chapter 6, we will talk more in depth about what the phrase "in a manner worthy" means in reference to our way of life and our calling or the gospel. For now, let us just understand that what Paul is saying here is that we are to conduct ourselves in a way that reflects the gospel of Christ. There are two particulars that he talks about here that I think are instructive to us.

First, we are to be standing firm. That is to say that we are not retreating from confrontation with the world. So many times, Christians seem so busy giving in to the expectations and standards of the world that we lose our ability to be salt and light or shine like stars. Truth is relevant, and we lose our relevance in the world when we fail to stand firm in the truth of God. Paul is calling us here to establish the standard of Christ and to stand firm on that standard.

Second, we are to be unified. We are to be of one mind and to be striving together. It makes sense that if we all have the mind of Christ and are all called according to His one purpose, we should be of one mind and be striving for the one faith of the gospel. Unity for unity's sake is a false notion. The Bible always teaches unity around the revealed nature and character of God, the person and work of Jesus, and the mandates of Scripture. When we have the singular focus Jesus had on the glory of God through the fulfillment of His mission, we will have unity with all those who have that same singular focus, as was the case with the followers of Christ in Acts, Chapter 2.

> *And they devoted themselves to the apostles' teaching and the fellowship, to the breaking of bread and the prayers. And awe came upon every soul, and many wonders and signs were being done through the apostles. And all who believed were together and had all things in common. And they were selling their possessions and belongings and distributing the proceeds to all, as any had need. And day by day, attending the temple together and breaking bread in their homes, they received their food with glad and generous hearts, praising God and having favor with all the people. And the Lord added to their number day by day those who were being saved.* ACTS 2:42–47 (ESV)

The result is that we conduct ourselves accordingly. We do not get caught up in the affairs of the world as Paul says in 2 Timothy 2:4, *"No soldier in active service entangles himself in the affairs of everyday life, so that he may please the one who enlisted him as a soldier."* The issue becomes what we can do to please God instead of what we can do to be successful in the world. We will think in terms of what is the best that I can do, not in terms of what is the least that I can get away with doing. We will see how close we can live to the standard of Christ, by the work of the Spirit, and not how close we can live to the standard of the world and still call ourselves Christians.

Throughout the rest of this book we will take a much more detailed look at how we can view ourselves as leaders and present ourselves as examples by being renewed in our attitudes, our thinking, and our conduct. However, we can see that as we remain true to the standard of Christ, others will see the standard of His life reflected in ours.

The essential questions are really very simple. They only require that we be completely honest before God. The trick is that He already knows the depth of our hearts and wants only for us to be real before Him. Is Christ your ultimate standard? Is He firmly established as Lord in your life? Do others see Him in you when they look to your life as a standard?

CHAPTER 2
INFLUENCE:
A Mandate to Lead

If you point these things out to the brothers, you will be a good minister of Christ Jesus, brought up in the truths of the faith and of the good teaching that you have followed. Have nothing to do with godless myths and old wives' tales; rather, train yourself to be godly. For physical training is of some value, but godliness has value for all things, holding promise for both the present life and the life to come. This is a trustworthy saying that deserves full acceptance (and for this we labor and strive), that we have put our hope in the living God, who is the Savior of all men, and especially of those who believe. Command and teach these things. Don't let anyone look down on you because you are young, but set an example for the believers in speech, in life, in love, in faith and in purity. 1 TIMOTHY 4:6–12

"Leadership is influence, the ability of one person to influence others."
      J. Oswald Sanders
      Spiritual Leadership

"Spiritual leadership is moving people onto God's agenda."
      Henry Blackabay
      Spiritual Leadership

There are few of us who view ourselves as leaders. There are even fewer of us who think of ourselves as spiritual leaders. When we think of the term "spiritual leader," we think of a pastor or priest, an evangelist or conference speaker, a worship leader or contemporary Christian artist. We see these people as different from ourselves, set apart somehow by their position, gift or calling.

In those ideas of calling, gifts, and position lie the root of much of our confusion. It is not the position of a pastor, evangelist, or worship leader that makes them a spiritual leader. Those titles are just positions that they hold, and while those positions do have certain requirements and qualifications attached to them, they bring with them only positional authority. That means the position has some inherent authority that comes along with it, like a police officer.

However, that positional authority does not make them spiritual leaders, only spiritual icons. Real spiritual leadership comes from being people with personal authority. Personal authority is the result of living a life of purpose, integrity, and vision that allows others to see God at work in you. Just like every one of us who is a believer in Christ has a spiritual gift, we each have a spiritual calling as well. That spiritual calling is to salvation by grace through faith in Christ, to go into all the world and make disciples, and to be an example of one who believes. Within that calling, God has a specific purpose for each one of us, but we all have a mandate to be and make disciples—a mandate to lead.

When 1 Timothy 4:12 tells us to *"set an example for the believers,"* that is exactly what God is calling us to do. Spiritual leadership is the ability to see where God is leading and how He intends to get there, teaching others to see the same thing, and showing them the way by example. The first thing that we have to see is that we all, as believers, have a mandate from God to be leaders on our campuses, in our homes, in our workplaces and in our churches— to be an example of one who believes.

What Is a Mandate?

A mandate is a transfer or delegation of authority. What it means to have a mandate is that one party, who holds authority, gives that authority to you in order to execute a particular role or assignment. It can be equated to when you were in elementary school, and the teacher would assign a classroom monitor when she left the room for a minute. Now, before that child was assigned to be monitor, he was just like all of the other children and had no authority over the others. However, when he was assigned by the teacher, she delegated her authority down to the child in order for him to fill the role of monitor and execute the duties of that role. Now, it is likely that this child would not have the same authority as the teacher because his personal authority is not the same. However, the teacher's personal authority will support the student until she returns.

In the same way, God has given each of us a mandate. God, who holds all the positional authority in the universe as the Creator of the universe, delegates to us a position of authority in Matthew 28 when He commissions us the position of authority to *"go into all the world, and make disciples."* He also holds all personal authority as the Savior of the world, and in 1 Timothy 4, He explains to us how to receive His mandate to be spiritual leaders by being examples of those who believe. So, a mandate is much more than a position or a title. Our mandate is a command from God, followed by a transferring of His power and His authority to us as believers to execute the responsibilities of the role of spiritual leader.

Train Yourself to Be Godly

We can see that there is a necessary process by which we receive a mandate. Though we are all called, commissioned, and even commanded to be examples spiritually, there is a process that we must go through in order to receive our mandate as spiritual leaders. We have an inherent position of authority as children of God, but it is by training ourselves to be godly that we become people of authority.

1 Timothy 4 tells us that we are to train ourselves to be godly because it has value in this life and the life to come. We well understand what the value of being godly will have in the life to come. When we stand before God in heaven, we will all desire to have lived godly lives. We know our good deeds cannot save us and that only the blood of Christ and His righteousness will purchase our way into eternity with God. However, there will also be that day when we are measured before the presence of God. He will reveal what He created and called us to be, as well as how far we fell short of that goal, His glory. Training ourselves to be godly will certainly have value on that day.

What we often forget is that training ourselves to be godly also has benefit for this life. It is only in godly living that we can gain access to all that God has stored up for us in heavenly places. It is only by training ourselves to be godly that we can live the abundant life that Jesus came to give, and only by being transformed that we can prove what the good, pleasing and perfect will of God is in our lives.

So we know that training comes with a reward both for this life and the life to come, but what does it mean to train ourselves to be godly? How do we do it? Exactly what does this verse imply in our lives?

First, training ourselves to be godly implies discipline. The analogy that Paul uses here is one of physical exercise. Anyone who has ever been an athlete or undertaken a physical training routine of any kind understands that the first thing that is required in training is discipline. Discipline is important because the results do not come immediately.

I am reminded of a popular television commercial where the

guy is in the gym getting ready to work out. He gets his headphones on and stretches a little and then steps on the scale. He appears motivated by what he sees and takes off running around the weight room. After only one lap, he returns to his position, seemingly exhausted, and steps back on the scale again. Of course there is no change and the man seems crushed. It takes hours and days of physical training to achieve a change in your body, and there are many days when we get discouraged or just do not feel like training. That is why we have to be disciplined to keep our commitment to training.

Training also implies discipline because there is more to training our bodies than exercise. If we are going to achieve a change in our bodies, we have to remove some things from our lifestyle, break bad habits, and make better choices. Some people are dedicated to getting up and going to the gym every day. However, they lack that same dedication when it comes to getting up and leaving the dinner table. Training implies discipline because it implies doing the things we know we need to do to achieve change and not doing the things we know keep us from achieving change.

The same is true for those of us who seek to train ourselves to be godly. Training implies discipline because we know that we are going to have to make hard changes and do things that we do not want to do or feel like doing. It is on those days when we cannot see a change and we lose sight of why we are training ourselves to be godly that we have to remain disciplined and hold fast to our commitment. Remember, it is the work you do today that will produce a change in your spiritual life in the weeks, months, and years to come.

Second, training ourselves to be godly implies hard work. That is like saying we are going to train ourselves physically to be a world class athlete or professional body builder. There is a long way between where we are now and where we desire to be. The thing that separates us from our goal is a lot of hard work.

Professional athletes do not just say that they want to be the best in the world at what they do and then wake up one day to that reality. They have to work hard to get where they desire to be, and then often, they have to work twice as hard to stay there. Why is it that we think it should be any different spiritually? Often, as Christians, we think because we say that we want to be like Christ or we want to be spiritual leaders, we can just say a prayer and wake up one day to that reality.

The truth is that it takes a lot of hard work for us to train ourselves to be godly. We have to get up and go to the gym every morning, and we have to eat right during the day. We have to stop the bad habits that hold up the change and make the hard decisions that are required. It is a labor of love, but a labor all the same. That is why the Bible uses terms like press, strive and labor.

Everywhere I go, I try to find an older believer who is respected and viewed as a spiritual leader. I like to ask them how they got to be so godly. Almost without exception, they all say the same thing. First, most of them will not view themselves as more godly than anyone else. Then, they will tell you that it did not happen overnight. Every godly elderly man or woman to whom I have ever asked that question responded in much the same way. "I got here one day at a time, getting up in the morning and getting on my knees." "It happened by reading God's Word and letting the Spirit work in my life." There are no spiritual shortcuts. Training yourself to be godly requires hard work.

Third, training yourself to be godly implies a desired outcome. Now this may seem simplistic but it is foundational. To train yourself to be godly implies that your ultimate goal is to be like Christ. A marathon runner trains to run marathons. A boxer trains to fight. A soldier trains for war. If we train ourselves, we must have a goal in mind. We must keep our standard ever in front of us and continue to strive to achieve that goal. The change we are looking for is a change in us, and it is for us to look more and more like

Christ. If you are training yourself to be godly so that you can be successful or popular, you are training for the wrong goal. If you are training yourself to be godly so that you can be like Christ, then you are on the right path. Our discipline and work do not make us godly, but they are the means that God has chosen to transform us and conform us to the image of Christ.

Put Your Hope in God

We know we train ourselves to be godly because it benefits both this life and the life to come. But why do we believe that godliness is the answer? Why do we discipline ourselves and do the hard work of becoming godly? Paul says that we labor and strive because *"we have put our hope in the living God."*

What does it really mean to have put our hope in the living God, and why would that cause us to choose such a difficult course? Hope is the key by-product of faith in our everyday lives and is a basic need of all mankind. Scripture says that without hope man would perish. This is true because if we had no hope there would be no reason to press on. The pressing question of life is, "Why?". Why am I here? Why did this happen to me? Why is life so hard? No matter what answer you give to the question, if there is no hope that there is purpose, or that tomorrow will be better than today, then your answer brings no comfort or peace. Without hope, we would all just lie in bed and dwell in atrophy until death.

As believers, we have hope. We have placed our hope in the living God because He is the savior of all mankind, and especially those who believe. We labor and strive to be like God because our hope is in Him and not in ourselves or in the things of this world. In fact, the reason so many of us find it hard to labor and strive to be godly is because we still reserve a little hope in ourselves or the things of this world.

If we are going to train ourselves to be godly, we have to lay aside all our hope in ourselves, our intellect, good looks and charm, and in the things of this world, in money, success, and popularity. If we are going to train ourselves to be godly, we have to hope in one thing and one thing alone: that God is who He says He is and can do what He says He can do. Otherwise, when we do not feel like being disciplined or doing the work, we will depend on other things to get us by and we will never achieve the change, the goal, that we desire—Christ-likeness.

Hope in God is more than just desire. Biblical hope is the assurance of things to come. To say that we have put our hope in God is not just to say we desire God to do something in our lives, like we desire a particular gift for Christmas. Hope is having the assurance that God has a plan for our lives, a good, pleasing and perfect will not to harm us but to prosper us, and that He who began a good work in us will see it through to completion. In short, hope is a belief in the promises of God.

The promises of God are the object of our hope. We labor and strive to be godly because we have hope in the promises of God. We know that God has never broken a promise to us and His promises to never leave us, to protect us, and to provide for our needs are as sure to us as any historical event. That is why we want to be godly, not because we must be in order for God to keep His promises, but because we know He will and that is the only hope we have.

Faith in the nature and character of God is the foundation of hope. We hope in the promises of God because of who God is. That is why Scripture is so important. That is where God has revealed His nature, character, and promises to us. We can have confidence in what God says because we know that He is always the same and has all the power in the universe to keep His promises. If we lose sight of who God is, then we will lose faith in the promises of God and therefore lose hope. The result is that we will stop laboring and striving to train ourselves to be godly. Because of the hope we have in God, we labor and strive, and train ourselves to be godly and to give an account for the hope that is in us.

Set an Example

Train yourselves to be godly, put your hope in the living God, and do not allow anyone to look down on you because you are young. Rather, set an example for the believers in speech, conduct, love, faith, and purity. The point here is that we are to be examples. Your leadership role at home, school, work, and church is not merely a future goal but an immediate command.

Paul says that regardless of our age, race or social standing, we are to influence people to be like Christ. That is why I believe that the phrase, *"do not let them look down on you because you are young,"* has a double meaning. The word that is translated here "young" or "youthfulness" is the same root word that Paul uses in Ephesians 4:20–24 for, *"to be **made new** in the attitude of your minds"* and to *"put on the **new** self, created to be like God in true righteousness and holiness."*

The Greek word is *neos* and it means "new," "young," or "youthful." I know Paul is writing to Timothy here and that Timothy was probably very young while he was leading the church at Ephesus. I believe Paul was encouraging Timothy not to let the people look down on him because of his age. However, I also believe that Paul chose this word very carefully because it also warns us to not let anyone despise us because we are a new creation. Instead, be an example of what newness is.

Influence is the ability to lead others in a new direction. As new creations in Christ, we are to be examples of what Christ is doing in those who believe. You were created and called for greatness. You are being conformed to the image and likeness of God. Do not let anyone look down on that. Do not let them push you to the back of the conversation just because you are a Christian. Do not let them laugh at your beliefs just because you are being transformed. Do not let them write you off as a conservative, right wing, religious fanatic just because you have placed your hope in the living God. Instead be a leader. Be an example! You are to be a person of spiritual influence in your sphere of life. Whether you are at school, at work, at home, or at church, you are to be a spiritual leader, an example.

This is not just a suggestion. Remember, this is a command and a mandate from God. How do we do it? God never calls us to anything that He does not give us instructions on how to achieve. In all my years as a youth minister, I tried never to teach what to do without teaching how. That is why I love Paul so much. He always gives us a list to instruct us on what to think about: speech, conduct, love, faith, and purity.

How do we set an example that leads people toward where God wants them to be? The first thing that we need to think about is our speech. Your speech is what comes out of your mouth, and I believe that Paul starts the list with speech because it so often forms the first impression people have of you. As we set an example for others, the words that we use and what we say we believe will be the first and often only impression people have of us. Therefore, our speech is to be godly. Paul gives us some insight into what that might look like in Ephesians 4 and 5.

> *Therefore each of you must put off falsehood and speak truthfully to his neighbor, for we are all members of one body. Do not let any unwholesome talk come out of your mouths, but only what is helpful for building others up according to their needs, that it may benefit those who listen.* EPHESIANS 4:25, 29 (NIV)

> *Nor should there be obscenity, foolish talk or coarse joking, which are out of place, but rather thanksgiving. Speak to one another with psalms, hymns and spiritual songs. Sing and make music in your heart to the Lord, always giving thanks to God the Father for everything, in the name of our Lord Jesus Christ.* EPHESIANS 5:4, 19–20 (NIV)

The second thing that Paul warns us to be mindful of as we labor and strive to be a godly example is our conduct. We all know that after someone gets to know us our words only have meaning or influence if our actions back them up. As people start to watch our lives as an example of one who believes, they will look to see if what we do matches what we say we believe. Our conduct is all of the actions of our physical body. As we set an example for others, what we do will be what solidifies their lasting impression. Therefore, our conduct must be godly. Once again, Paul gives us some basic instructions in this area of our life in Ephesians.

> *And do not grieve the Holy Spirit of God, with whom you were sealed for the day of redemption. Get rid of all bitterness, rage and anger, brawling and slander, along with every form of malice. Be kind and compassionate to one another, forgiving each other, just as in Christ God forgave you.* EPHESIANS 4:30–32 (NIV)

> *But among you there must not be even a hint of sexual immorality, or of any kind of impurity, or of greed, because these are improper for God's holy people. For you were once darkness, but now you are light in the Lord. Live as children of light (for the fruit of the light consists in all goodness, righteousness and truth) and find out what pleases the Lord. Have nothing to do*

with the fruitless deeds of darkness, but rather expose them. For it is shameful even to mention what the disobedient do in secret. But everything exposed by the light becomes visible, for it is light that makes everything visible. This is why it is said:

"Wake up, O sleeper,
rise from the dead,
and Christ will shine on you."

Be very careful, then, how you live—not as unwise but as wise, making the most of every opportunity, because the days are evil. Therefore do not be foolish, but understand what the Lord's will is. Do not get drunk on wine, which leads to debauchery. Instead, be filled with the Spirit. EPHESIANS 5:3, 8–18 (NIV)

The third thing we are instructed to be mindful of is the desire of our hearts, or love. Truthfully, our words are the first impression people have of who we are, and what we do gives credibility to that or takes credibility from that and serves as a more lasting impression. But, with that said, what really concerns God is our heart. That is why the greatest commandment, as Jesus gives it in Matthew 23, is not about speech or conduct, but about love.

There are a lot of people in our churches who say all of the right things and do all of the right things but they do them for the wrong reasons. Though they "talk the talk" and "walk the walk," their motivations are not grounded in a pure love for God. Paul warned Timothy about these people in 2 Timothy 3:2 when he said, *"People will be lovers of themselves, lovers of money, boastful, proud, abusive, disobedient to their parents, ungrateful, unholy, without love, unforgiving, slanderous, without self-control, brutal, not lovers of the good, treacherous, rash, conceited, lovers of pleasure rather than lovers of God—having a form of godliness but denying its power."* God is not so much concerned with what we do or what we say as much as

He is concerned with the motivation of our hearts—who we love and serve.

It is the desire of our hearts that God is ultimately after. He wants us to desire Him and delight ourselves in Him above anything else in the world. Psalm 37:4 says, *"Delight yourself in the Lord and he will give you the desires of your heart."* God wants to give us what we desire most. The key is that what we desire most must be Him. That is why Christ died, to bring us to God. To desire anything else more is to devalue the work of Christ. That is why He tells us in Matthew 6:33, *"But seek first His kingdom and His righteousness, and all these things will be added to you."*

Paul is telling us that if we want to be examples and people of spiritual influence, it is not only about what we say and do, it is also about what we love. What is the object of the desire of our hearts? If it is wealth or fame, position or popularity, then we are striving for the wrong things and we are lovers of ourselves more than we are lovers of God. However, Paul is not through with his list, and the Spirit is not through digging deeper into our lives.

The fourth thing that we are instructed to take note of, if we are going to be examples of those who believe, is our faith. Now we talk a great deal about faith in the church, but I often wonder if we think a great deal about what it is. Wayne Grudem, in his *Systematic Theology*, defines saving faith as, "trust in Jesus as a living person for forgiveness of sins and for eternal life with God." He emphasizes, "[F]aith is not just a belief in facts but personal trust in Jesus to save me." Trust is the real understanding here. In our modern vocabulary, you can believe something and even have faith in it without having any real commitment to it. The biblical understanding of faith is complete trust in the person of Jesus.

Faith is the reality of trust, and we trust in many things. We put our faith in our social status, our financial status, or our good looks and charm or intelligence. We say and do all the right things and even do them mostly out of a love for God, but in the everyday push-comes-to-shove of our lives, we place our faith, our trust, and therefore our hope in everything else in this world before God. I have been involved in more situations than I care to recount where churches that love God put their trust more in the wisdom of men than in God. I believe that God is more concerned about where the weight of your trust lies than He is even about your motivation and deeds, because your motivation and deeds cannot remain true if your trust is not in God.

> *Do not let kindness and truth leave you; bind them around your neck, write them on the tablet of your heart. So you will find favor and good repute in the sight of God and man.* **Trust in the LORD with all your heart** *and do not lean on your own understanding. In all your ways acknowledge Him, and He will make your paths straight. Do not be wise in your own eyes; Fear the LORD and turn away from evil.* PROVERBS 3:3–7

As Paul digs deeper into our lives, we realize that his list is a progression deeper and deeper into the depths of our soul. And so when we get to the end of our list and we see purity, it causes us to pause. When we talk about purity in the church, especially in youth groups, we often boil it down to, or focus on, sexual purity. Now that is an important topic that we should discuss, teach and preach; however, it is not what Paul means by purity in this context.

We already established that conduct included all of the acts of the physical body and even used Ephesians 5:3 as one of our reference verses for conduct. So, sexual purity and all manners of moral purity would have been covered by Paul in the second item on his list. What then does he mean here by purity? He means what most of the Bible means by purity when it does not qualify the term. Purity is the depth of wholeness.

Pure means to be one hundred percent of a thing with no

contamination of another thing mixed in. Pure water is H_2O with nothing else mixed in. That is what God is concerned about here. More than our speech, our conduct, the desire of our hearts, or the object of our trust, God knows the real issue is our purity of heart because it is the key to intimate fellowship with God and real godliness. Psalm 24:3–4 makes this point very clear when it asks, *"Who may ascend the hill of the Lord? Who may stand in His holy place? He who has clean hands and a pure heart, who does not lift his soul to an idol or swear by what is false."* Purity is an issue of the heart that insists that we must be all about godliness, with no idols. Then, as Matthew 5 says, we will see God.

Purity, godliness, and absolute integrity of the heart is God's goal in our lives. It is His will for us that we be like Christ. If we are going to be examples of those who believe, we must set our hearts on God alone. In the depths of our soul, there must be a wholeness and purity that is deeper and richer than what we do or say. The foundation of all of our motivation and trust is purity of heart. For as Titus 1:15 says, *"To the pure, all things are pure, but to those who are corrupted and do not believe, nothing is pure. In fact, both their minds and consciences are corrupted."*

So then, we have a calling from God to be spiritual leaders in our sphere of influence, whatever it might be. In order to do that, we must be mindful of our words and conversations, we must be mindful of our conduct and physical actions. More than anything, we must be mindful of our own hearts. What is the object of our love? Where do we ultimately place our trust? Deep down in the deepest depths of our soul, who are we? Don't miss the point. You have been taught all your life what to do and what not to do. Somehow, you have become convinced that is what being a good Christian is all about. But it is not entirely about those things. In fact it is primarily about something much deeper, a relationship with your creator—God. It is about the desire of your heart and the object of your faith and hope, and who God created and called you to be.

Words and actions and thoughts flow out of that, but the issue is who we are before God.

> *Dear friends, now we are children of God, and what we will be has not yet been made known. But we know that when he appears, we shall be like him, for we shall see him as he is. Everyone who has this hope in him purifies himself, just as he is pure.* 1 JOHN 3: 2–3 (NIV)

IMPACT

Mr. John Hicks is a man who first influenced my life as a board member at Southern Seminary when I was a student there. He impacted my life because he was also a member and deacon at Elk Creek Baptist Church where I served as a youth minister during seminary. I knew a lot about John Hicks and his accomplishments. I experienced him and his wife being godly people and their love for God. They loved me and my wife like we were their own children, and I saw him stand firm like granite through many changes, trials and battles.

After leaving Kentucky, I stayed in contact with Mr. John and Mrs. Emma as much as possible, and they continued to have a lasting impact on my life. Just months before he passed away, we visited them in their home. Mr. John opened up his library and told me to take what I wanted. It was one of the hardest gifts I had ever received. When I hesitated to take more than just a volume or two, he told me to take what I wanted because he would not need them. I knew what he meant, and I understood it was his way of having a lasting impact on my life. When Mr. John died, I was unable to go to the funeral and it broke my heart. A short while after, I was visiting some friends from that old church and one of them handed me Mr. John's obituary. I would like to share portions of it with you as an example of a life of impact.

John G. Hicks, 90, Elk Creek, KY, formerly of Jeffersontown, passed away Friday, November 5, 2004, at Baptist Hospital East, after a courageous struggle with cancer.

Born October 6, 1914, in Louisville, Mr. Hicks attended Male High School and the University of Louisville. In 1938, he earned his law degree from U of L and entered the practice of law with the firm Boehl, Stopher, Graves, and Deindoerpher in Louisville.

On May 29, 1941, he married Emma May Guynes, with whom he would share the remaining 64 years of his life. In 1942, he entered the US Army and was assigned to a medical detachment in France soon after D-Day.

After the war, Mr. Hicks returned to law practice. In 1963, he entered private practice and continued to practice law until shortly before his death.

Mr. Hicks was a devoted Christian and served as a deacon over the years for Deer Park Baptist, Davis Memorial Baptist, Cedar Creek Baptist, Living Hope Baptist, and Elk Creek Baptist Churches. A believer in the special role of the Jewish people in the Lord's work, Mr. Hicks served as a secretary and board member of the International Ministry to Israel, Inc., from 1955 until 1997.

In the 1960s, Mr. Hicks was instrumental in the founding of Baptist Homes for the Elderly. He was serving as the vice president of its board of directors at the time of his death. He and his wife were designated church messengers to the

Southern Baptist Convention on several occasions and he served on the convention's Committee on Boards and Committee on Committees during a critical period during the 1980s. In 1988, Mr. Hicks was named to the Board of Trustees of the Southern Baptist Theological Seminary and served as the board's secretary from 1990 to 1998. From 1999 to his death, he served as a board member of the Southern Seminary Foundation.

Mr. Hicks was a devoted member of the Louisville Northeast Camp of Gideons International since 1974, helping in the distribution of Bibles.

He was preceded in death by his parents...

He is survived by his wife, Emma; sister, three sons, and two grandsons.[2]

Mr. John was a man of integrity, insight, imitation and intensity. His life stands as an example of one who believes and its impact in the lives of many is clear. It is not his accomplishments and activities, as many and honorable as they are, that make Mr. Hicks' life one of impact. What makes his life one of impact is the effect so much of what he was a part of had on my life and the lives of so many others. So much so that someone thought so much of the impact that he had in their life to save his obituary and show it to me, and I think so much of the impact that he had on my life to want to share a piece of it with you.

---

[2] "Obituaries; Louisville, Southern Indiana and Regional Area Deaths" The Courier Journal, Louisville, Kentucky. 11/07/2004; page 6b.

CHAPTER 3
INTEGRITY:
Character Determines Impact

Hearing that Jesus had silenced the Sadducees, the Pharisees got together. One of them, an expert in the law, tested him with this question: "Teacher, which is the greatest commandment in the Law?" Jesus replied: "'Love the Lord your God with all your heart and with all your soul and with all your mind.' This is the first and greatest commandment. And the second is like it: 'Love your neighbor as yourself.' All the Law and the Prophets hang on these two commandments."
MATTHEW 22:34–40

"Good character is more to be praised than outstanding talent. Most talents are to some extent a gift. Good character, by contrast, is not given to us. We have to build it piece by piece—by thought, choice, courage, and determination."
        John Luther

There is a lot that we can learn from Matthew 22. However, as we saw in the last chapter, one of the primary things God desires for our lives is that we be pure. God wants us to be one hundred percent His with no mixture of anything else. The first of the Ten

Commandments reflects this chief desire of God when He tells us in Exodus 20:2–6, "*I am the LORD your God, who brought you out of the land of Egypt, out of the house of slavery. You shall have no other gods before me. You shall not make for yourself an idol, or any likeness of what is in heaven above or on the earth beneath or in the water under the earth. You shall not worship them or serve them; for I, the LORD your God, am a jealous God, visiting the iniquity of the fathers on the children, on the third and the fourth generations of those who hate Me, but showing loving-kindness to thousands, to those who love Me and keep My commandments.*"

When the religious leaders of the day questioned Jesus as to which command was the greatest, He gave them this first command to love God that they would have easily accepted, because they were experts at giving that outward appearance. However, Jesus also revealed their hypocrisy by coupling it with a second command for which they did not ask, nor were they prepared. Love the Lord with all that you are and love you neighbor as yourself. The implication is that our love for God will reveal itself in the way that we love other people. The key thing that we see then in Matthew 22 is that there is supposed to be a consistency or wholeness in our lives. We are not supposed to be compartmentalized or hold a belief in one area of life and have it not effect every other area of our lives. That is the essence of a Christian worldview, that we view every area of life through the reality of God in our lives. Our love for God should affect every area of our lives and prove itself in our relationships with others. The word here is integrity. Once we have the integrity of the heart that we discussed in Chapter 2, it should begin to work itself out in every area of our lives.

What Is Integrity?

Integrity is the state of being complete or unified. Webster's Dictionary describes it as "intactness, firmness of character." To help us get a better understanding of the true meaning of the word, I will use an illustration from my friend Randy Bruner. He points out that the root word is integer. An integer is a whole number, and thus the idea of purity as the depth of wholeness or wholeness at the deepest level is very important to understanding integrity. That purity, or wholeness, should reveal itself in wholeness of character, and character determines our impact as examples.

In the last chapter, we talked about our calling to be examples as a mandate from God to use our influence to lead people from where they are to where God wants them to be. Influence, however, does not always have a lasting effect. We can come into contact with someone only once or twice and have an influence on them. I have been influenced many times in my life by people I did not really know or had not even met. The truth of the matter is that influence, more often than not, has a short-term effect.

When we talk about purity of heart and integrity, we are talking about the factors that take our example as believers from being a short-term influence to a long-term impact.

It is the personal authority that we gain by being people of integrity that causes our influence to work in a person's life over a long period of time. As they see our lives and are drawn to Christ living in us, they will begin to watch more and more closely to determine the depth of the reality of our wholeness. When we are able to demonstrate through our actions, over time, that there is a reality to what we appear to be, we will begin to have a lasting impact on their lives.

All things prove themselves over time. That is one of the fundamental principles of life. The Bible says that you reap what you sow. If you plant a watermelon seed, you will get a watermelon every time. If you plant a corn seed, you will get corn. If you ever plant a watermelon seed and get corn, you let me know, because you have just broken a fundamental law of nature and life. What is inside is what will eventually come out. People may be influenced by the fact that we look like a watermelon seed, but they will be impacted by the reality that we produce watermelons.

The third level is legacy. That is the focus of Chapters 8–9 of this book. For now, we need to understand that it is in the legacy that we leave behind that the real truth about our purity, wholeness, and integrity is understood. Our impact as examples is most real when it becomes generational. That is why God has established the family, so that our faith is passed down from generation to generation as parents serve as the primary spiritual influence in the lives of their children. They are influenced by our being seeds, impacted by our producing fruit, but we have left a legacy when our fruit produces seeds that can be planted to continue the process.

A thing is sometimes best understood by negating concepts, or knowing its opposite. Another word that comes from the root integer is integrate, which means to bring together into a whole or make complete. We can see the connection. The opposite of integrate is disintegrate, which means to separate into elements or blow apart. Not allowing our love for God to affect every area of our lives by trying to keep our life in different compartments and separating our faith from other areas is like strapping a bomb to ourselves as examples. Compartmentalization of our lives leads to the disintegration of our lives.

Integrity is a wholeness that results from bringing together every area of our lives in absolute obedience to the will of God. It is a consistency of character in every compartment and every area of life. A person of integrity does not have divided passions, nor do they have divided trust: they are one hundred percent real. They love God with all of their heart, soul, mind, and strength.

The Importance of Integrity

It is easy to see the importance of integrity when we understand that compartmentalization and disintegration go hand in hand.

However, there are a few keys points about the importance of integrity as it relates to our calling as spiritual leaders that I think will help us as we think about building integrity into our lives.

We must understand that integrity, though it is not always easy, is a positive thing. God does not call us to be holy to keep us from having fun. God calls us to be holy so that we will be set apart for Him to use. God wants us to have purity of heart so that we will not be double minded, not so we will be closed minded. God wants us to have wholeness and integrity because it brings peace and it sets us free to be what God created and called us to be. The Greek philosopher Socrates had it right when he said, "The first key to greatness is to be in reality what you appear to be."

Secondly, it is important for us to see that not only does integrity qualify us as examples, but a lack of integrity disqualifies us. 1 Samuel 2:30 says, "*Therefore the LORD, the God of Israel, declares: 'I promised that your house and your father's house would minister before me forever.' But now the LORD declares: 'Far be it from me! Those who honor me I will honor, but those who despise me will be disdained.'*" Without integrity, we are disqualified as examples.

That is why we have so much trouble witnessing to our friends and sharing our faith at home, school, and work. Because we have a lack of integrity, we are left with a lack of influence and with no real impact. We have compartmentalized God into the religious area of our lives, and the other areas are disintegrating before the eyes of those around us.

This is also why so many lost people view the church as useless to them. In their view, the church has lost its moral authority, lost its identity, and been separated into elements (disintegrated), instead of being unified and made whole. This is largely the result of the churches' attempt to be culturally blended. In our attempt to be culturally relevant, we have sacrificed the truth of the gospel. Our integrity rests in God's revealed truth, and His truth will always be relevant to His creation. We must be people of wholeness and integrity if God is going to do something revolutionary through us!

Developing Integrity

John Maxwell says, "Integrity is not so much what we do as who we are." There is great deal of truth in that statement, because integrity comes from wholeness, and wholeness comes from purity of heart, and purity of heart has little to do with activity and everything to do with a relationship with God. However, integrity is not something that comes naturally. Like almost every aspect of our spiritual growth, it is something that we have to set out to develop intentionally.

The first thing that we have to understand if we are going to develop a life of integrity is that integrity requires effort. That is to say, in order to have wholeness and to achieve that synergy that comes from inner unity and purity there are things that we must do. These are not outward activities that have to do with reputation, but inward spiritual disciplines that have to do with real character. Therefore, developing integrity has to do with developing spiritual disciplines such as reading Scripture, prayer, fellowship with other believers, giving, and ministry.

John Luther says, "Good character is more to be praised than outstanding talent. Most talents are to some extent a gift. Good character by contrast, is not given to us. We have to build it piece by piece—by thought, choice, courage and determination." I love to talk with older believers, such as Mr. Hicks, who have lived a godly life and have so much wisdom to share about how to be who God created and called us to be. When I talk with these older saints, one thing always strikes me. None of these mighty believers became godly men or women overnight. Every one will tell you that it happens day by day, over a lifetime, by prayer and reading the Word. You cannot just say that you want to be godly and have a life of integrity, and one day wake up and that is the case. You have to work out your salvation and receive your sanctification, through a process of giving up what God asks for and receiving what God provides. If it were easy, everyone would live lives of integrity, but they do not because it requires hard work.

The next thing we need to see is that integrity involves entirety. We have already talked about the fact that integrity has to do with wholeness and bringing every area of your life together in unity and submission to Christ. This not only means bringing all of the external compartments of your life together, but it also involves every aspect of your inner life. If we are going to love God with all of our heart, soul, mind, and strength, then integrity involves what you love, believe, think and do.

Integrity involves what you love because we are commanded to love God with all of our hearts. What we love is an issue in integrity because we are to be one hundred percent surrendered to God. The first area of surrender must be the desires of our hearts. What do you love? For most of us, there is something we love. It may be a rival, or even an idol, that competes with God for our affection. It may be another person, a habit, a style of music, or social status that we love more than God, but we know we love it more than God because we are not willing to give it up for God. That is why idolatry is the most talked about issue in Scripture.

God wants to be the chief desire of our hearts, and He wants to give us every other desire of our hearts if we will just desire Him first and most of all. The Bible puts it this way in Psalm 37:4, *"Delight yourselves in the Lord, and He will give you the desires of your heart."* Maybe we are more familiar with the concept as communicated in Matthew 6:33 *"But seek first His kingdom and His righteousness, and all these things will be added to you."* Integrity involves loving God with all of our hearts.

Integrity involves what you believe because we are commanded to love God with all of our souls. In our soul is where our faith, hope, and trust reside. So many of us, who do believe in God, do not have integrity in our soul because God is not the object of all our faith, hope, and trust. When push comes to shove and life gets really hard, where do we place our faith? Who or what do we trust when we are in a jam? When we dream, for what are we hoping?

God wants us to place all of our faith in Him, to believe in Him above anything else. He wants us to hope for the things that He has promised and to trust in His promises as absolutely enough in our lives. I know that we all need someone to lean on, someone we can trust. But where do we go first? Do we trust in our friends, our family, our social status, or our financial strength more than God? Do we depend on the things of this world, or do we put all of our faith in God? We are to invest all of our soul in our relationship with God. Integrity involves loving God with all your soul.

Integrity involves what you think because we are commanded to love God with all our minds. What does it mean to love God with all of your mind? I am sure I cannot comprehend what all it means, but I know it means that I am to study God's word and all of my thoughts are to center around God. That means that I must control what comes into my mind. 2 Corinthians 10:5 says, *"We are destroying speculations and every lofty thing raised up against the knowledge of God, and we are taking every thought captive to the obedience of Christ."* I must also work to put positive things into my mind. Philippians 4:8–9 says, *"Finally, brothers, whatever is true, whatever is noble, whatever is right, whatever is pure, whatever is lovely, whatever is admirable—if anything is excellent or praiseworthy—think about such things. Whatever you have learned or received or heard from me, or seen in me—put it into practice. And the God of peace will be with you."*

That is why I try never to tell students what to listen to or watch, but instead I try to teach them the principles that will allow them to make good decisions about how they think. You cannot love God with all your mind if you are allowing your thoughts to be dominated and dictated by the things of the world. Instead of pounding students with do's and don'ts, we have to be about teaching them how to love God with their minds. We have to learn to dwell on the things of God and to work hard at thinking about God. When I work hard at thinking about God, it causes my entire being to be focused on Him. Then I am beginning to have integrity of mind. Integrity involves loving God with all of your mind.

Integrity involves what you do because we are commanded to love God with all our strength. First, we are to be strong. So often we hear how we are to be passive and humble, but those attributes are not in opposition with true strength. Strength is power under control. That is a great picture of God. Humility is not thinking less of yourself, but thinking of yourself less. We are commanded to be both humble and strong. Eleven times in the Bible we are told to be strong and courageous. Every other command is made possible by this strength that comes from God. Our dependence and faith in that strength is where true courage comes from. We are to be strong and love God with all our strength. Everything we do requires our strength, and therefore all we do should be out of a love for God. 1 Corinthians 10:31 says, *"Whether, then, you eat or drink or whatever you do, do all to the glory of God."* If we have integrity in every area of our lives, the integrity of what we do will take care of itself as an overflow of what is inside. Integrity involves loving God with all of your strength.

The final key for us to understand is that integrity results in excellence. God created and called us for greatness. We are created in the image of God and are now being conformed to the likeness of Christ. If we develop true integrity in our lives, that wholeness and unity of being will set us free to be what God created and called us to be—like Christ. We have been called by God to be just like Christ, and if we could pull our lives together in unity and submission to the plan of God—if we could love God with all our heart, soul mind and strength—just think how great we could be.

Think of the level of excellence at which we could live our lives if we could just pull it all together. If we took the effort to train ourselves to love God more than anything else in this world, how cool would that be? We could be just like Christ! You will only become what you are becoming right now. If we develop integrity in our lives, we will be becoming like Christ.

CHAPTER 4
INTEGRITY:
Five Biblical Relationships

"Do not arouse or awaken love until it so desires."
SONG OF SOLOMON 2:7

"The world can do almost anything as well or better than the church. You need not be a Christian to build houses, feed the hungry, or heal the sick. There is only one thing the world cannot do. It cannot offer grace."
Gordon MacDonald

Song of Solomon 2:7 tells us, *"Do not arouse or awaken love until it so desires."* This principle is presented to help us have integrity in our relationships. Integrity in relationships is basically living out in your relationships to others the reality that you really believe what you say you do. Matthew 22 serves as a baseline, a summary of how what we believe should affect our relationships with other people. However, do our relationships fully reflect the truth of this verse?

Love—everyone wants it, everyone tries to find it. Yet, the pursuit of it has caused more heartache and pain, more brokenness and bitterness than all disease and war combined. We all struggle to understand love, but we far too often set ourselves up for a fall because we do not understand what love is and what it is not. We do not know what it means to love biblically. We confuse love with other experiences and emotions, and therefore have no basis to evaluate our relationships. We need a realistic and biblical understanding of love and relationships. We need an external and eternal standard by which we can evaluate our relationships. The Bible provides that standard.

Biblical Relationships

There are five primary biblical love relationships that we can use to help us measure and evaluate our relationships. The first of these is found in Matthew 5:43–45. *"You have heard that it was said, 'you shall love your neighbor and hate your enemy.' But I say to you, love your enemies and pray for those who persecute you, so that you may be sons of your Father who is in heaven; for He causes His sun to rise on the evil and the good, and sends rain on the righteous and the unrighteous."* Jesus himself commands us to love our enemies.

Who are our enemies? We know that our battle is not against flesh and blood, but against spiritual forces. The Bible never refers to anyone as our enemy for personal reasons. The only time we are to view someone as our enemy is when they stand in opposition to the things of God, or as Jesus says here, they persecute us for our faith. Even though they persecute us and stand against the things of God, we are to love them. We would often be wise to avoid them, and we would obviously not have the same relationship or fellowship with them that we would have with a neighbor or a brother, but we are to love them.

The second biblical love relationship is found in Leviticus 19:18 and is quoted in one of our key passages for integrity. *"Do not seek revenge or bear a grudge against one of your people, but love your neighbor as yourself. I am the LORD."* Jesus himself commands us to love our neighbors.

Who are our neighbors? Jesus was asked the same question

when He gave us this command in Luke 10. He responded by telling a story in verses 30–37.

> *Jesus replied and said, "A man was going down from Jerusalem to Jericho, and fell among robbers, and they stripped him and beat him, and went away leaving him half dead. And by chance a priest was going down on that road, and when he saw him, he passed by on the other side. Likewise a Levite also, when he came to the place and saw him, passed by on the other side. But a Samaritan, who was on a journey, came upon him; and when he saw him, he felt compassion, and came to him and bandaged up his wounds, pouring oil and wine on them; and he put him on his own beast, and brought him to an inn and took care of him. On the next day he took out two denarii and gave them to the innkeeper and said, 'Take care of him; and whatever more you spend, when I return I will repay you.' Which of these three do you think proved to be a neighbor to the man who fell into the robbers' hands?'" And he said, "The one who showed mercy toward him." Then Jesus said to him, "Go and do the same."*

Jesus' story illustrates that our neighbors are all those around us who are in need, or anyone to whom you may show mercy. Phillip Yancey, in his book, *What's So Amazing About Grace*, points out that this is the one thing that we as children of God have to offer the world that the world cannot duplicate, when he quotes Gordon MacDonald. "The world can do almost anything as well or better than the church. You need not be a Christian to build houses, feed the hungry, or heal the sick. There is only one thing the world cannot do. It cannot offer grace."[3] Though we may not

---

[3] Gordon MacDonald: Phillip Yancey, What's So Amazing About Grace? Grand Rapids: Zondervan, 1997, p.15.

be able to develop a deep relationship with all the people in need around us, we are commanded to display mercy, grace, to love them.

The third biblical love relationship is presented in John 13:34–35. *"A new commandment I give to you, that you love one another, even as I have loved you, that you also love one another. By this all men will know that you are My disciples, if you have love for one another."* Jesus himself gives us this new command to love our spiritual family.

Who are our spiritual family? Once again, Jesus gives us a very clear answer to this question when His earthly family came to get Him while He was teaching, in Matthew 12:48–50. *"But Jesus answered the one who was telling Him and said, 'Who is My mother and who are My brothers?' And stretching out His hand toward His disciples, He said, 'Behold My mother and My brothers! For whoever does the will of My Father who is in heaven, he is My brother and sister and mother.'"* Jesus makes it clear that our spiritual family are those who do the will of God. As adopted children of God, our spiritual family consists of all those, regardless of denomination or theological persuasion, who also have been adopted into His family. We may not enjoy being around them, have the same preferences as them, or even always agree with them, but it is abundantly clear that we are to love them.

The fourth biblical love relationship is explained by Paul in his letter to the Ephesians. In Ephesians 5:25–33, Paul commands us to love our spouses as a model of Christ's relationship with the church.

> *Husbands, love your wives, just as Christ also loved the church and gave Himself up for her, so that He might sanctify her, having cleansed her by the washing of water with the word, that He might present to Himself the church in all her glory, having no spot or wrinkle or*

any such thing; but that she would be holy and blameless. So husbands ought also to love their own wives as their own bodies. He who loves his own wife loves himself; for no one ever hated his own flesh, but nourishes and cherishes it, just as Christ also does the church, because we are members of His body. For this reason a man shall leave his father and mother and shall become joined to his wife, and the two shall become one flesh. This mystery is great; but I am speaking with reference to Christ and the church. Nevertheless, each individual among you also is to love his own wife even as himself, and the wife must see to it that she respects her husband.

Our spouse is that person to whom we have committed our lives and with whom we have become one. We are to love them as Christ loves the church; sacrificially, putting their spiritual well-being equal to our own, taking responsibility before God for their spiritual condition. We are to love them as our own bodies; provisionally, putting their physical needs above our own, taking responsibility before God for their physical condition. We are to love them as ourselves; caringly, putting their mental and emotional needs above our own, taking responsibility before God for their mental and emotional state. We may not feel emotionally romantic about them, but Christ himself demonstrates to us that we are to love them unconditionally.

The final and most important biblical love relationship can be found throughout Scripture. However, it is explicitly given to us in Deuteronomy 6 and repeated by Jesus in Matthew 22. Deuteronomy 6:4–5 says, "*Hear, O Israel: The Lord our God, the Lord is one. Love the Lord your God with all your heart and with all your soul and with all your strength.*" God himself commands us to love Him above all.

Five Implications

Now that we have an understanding of the five biblical love relationships, we need to see that there are five resulting implications from these that we can apply in helping us evaluate our relationships. First, the chief end of loving your enemy is to show God's provision for them. We are to pray for them because God brings both sun and rain to both the good and the evil. Second, the chief end of loving your neighbor is to display God's love to them in salvation. We are to want God's best for them, just as we do for ourselves and, like the Good Samaritan, display God's mercy and grace to them. Third, the chief end of loving our spiritual family is to demonstrate the love God has for His children. This is how they will know that we are God's children, because of the love they see us share. Fourth, the chief end of loving your spouse is to demonstrate physical, emotional, mental and spiritual intimacy. We represent the covenant relationship God has made with His people. Finally, the chief end of loving God is to display His glory. This elective love is the highest level of love. We cannot move from level to level without taking responsibility for the increased implications of those love relationships. We cannot cross over the lines of biblical love relationships without causing confusion and ultimately hurt.

What Love Is Not

Now that we have some understanding of what love is, it will help us maintain integrity in our relationships to discuss what love is not. 1 Corinthians 13 gives us a clear picture of the characteristics that make up love. By comparing those to the other expressions that we often confuse for love, we can identify clearly what love is not.

There are four main expressions that our society often confuse for love; lust, romance, infatuation, and sex. We often confuse love and lust when we speak of love as an appetite, because that is exactly what lust is—a strong appetite. It is an animal instinct of the flesh just like hunger. However, it is of a very different nature than love. While 1 Corinthians shows us that love is giving and focuses on the other person, lust takes and is always focused on fulfilling itself. We also see that love endures. Yet lust is not eternal and always subsides or changes its object. Therefore, while love is generous, enduring and fulfilling, lust is selfish, fleeting and empty. Like a wolf, it can never be satisfied.

We often confuse love and romance when we speak of love as an affair, a fantasy, or a fairytale, because that is exactly what romance is—a fanciful feeling. We see in 1 Corinthians that love keeps no record of wrongs suffered and it endures to the end. We all know that our feelings do not endure and fantasies do not deal much with wrongs suffered. Romance can certainly be part of love and it is a great thing to feel like you are in love, but romance has a very different character than does love. While love is a bond that exists out of a relationship, romance is a feeling that can be created. Love is the result of a decision and a commitment, while romance is the result of environment and circumstances. Love has no hidden agenda but is fully known. Romance is always a means to an end.

We often confuse love and infatuation when we speak of love as a crush or an obsession, because that is exactly what an infatuation is—acting foolishly out of delight. Now, we have already talked about how we are to delight ourselves in the Lord. This has to do with the desires of our hearts and in what our hearts delight. Therefore, there should be an obvious problem with our acting foolishly out of delight in another person. Infatuation is a strong fascination or intense interest, while love is a commitment. We certainly can have an interest in people and it is natural to be fascinated by the opposite sex. However, love should never cause us to act foolishly; love done God's way is never dangerous.

We often confuse love for sex when we talk about love as physical attraction, because that is exactly what sex is. Webster's Dictionary defines sex as, "activities, thoughts, etc., as influenced by the reproductive system." It obviously has a very different nature than does love. Sex is an act that is instinctive, effortless, and instant, while love is a process that is learned, requires attention and develops over time. We confuse sex and love when we confuse the intensity of sex with the intimacy of love. Sex outside of God's design of a covenant relationship (marriage) dulls a relationship and requires only physical interaction. 1 Corinthians 6:18–20 says, *"Flee from sexual immorality. All other sins a man commits are outside his body, but he who sins sexually sins against his own body. Do you not know that your body is a temple of the Holy Spirit, who is in you, whom you have received from God? You are not your own; you were bought at a price. Therefore honor God with your body."*

Love deepens a relationship and requires spiritual interaction. 1 Corinthians 13:10–13 says, *"But when the perfect comes, the partial will be done away. When I was a child, I used to speak like a child, think like a child, reason like a child; when I became a man, I did away with childish things. For now we see in a mirror dimly, but then face to face; now I know in part, but then I will know fully just as I also have been fully known. But now faith, hope, love, abide these three; but the greatest of these is love."* True love requires spiritual interaction because God is love and therefore all things that are true love come from God. Outside of God, we cannot know true love.

Because of our confusion or lack of understanding about love, there are three contexts of "love" in our culture. The first context of love is "love if." This is a context of love that says, "If you love me, you will . . ." or "I'll love you if you . . ." This is a conditional love that is bound to expectations that we must meet. This is not a love for us, but a love of what we can provide. The second context of love is "love because." This is a context of love that says, "I love you because you . . ." or, "Because you . . . I love you." This is a conditional love that is bound to performance or appearance. This is not a love of who we are, but a love of what we do or what we look like.

Now we can express our appreciation for what someone provides, does, or even looks like. However, we should never tie our love of someone to those things or allow someone's love for us to be tied to them. That is the context of true love, or "love period." This love is unconditional, all about giving, and the only biblical love. It is based on a commitment. Although it should involve our emotions, it is not primarily a feeling. Although it should engage our actions, it is not necessarily an activity. This love is evident when the happiness, health and spiritual growth of the other person is as important to us as our own and ours is as important to them as their own. 2 Corinthians instructs us;

> *Do not be bound together with unbelievers; for what partnership have righteousness and lawlessness, or what fellowship has light with darkness? Or what harmony has Christ with Belial, or what has a believer in common with an unbeliever? Or what agreement has the temple of God with idols? For we are the temple of the living God; just as God said.* 2 CORINTHIANS 6:14–16A

Not less important, not more important, but equally important. We are commanded to love only God more than ourselves, and we are commanded to love our spouses as Christ loves the church. We are to love everyone else equally as we love ourselves. That means that we want what is best for them in every way.

Young men, you should not say "I love you" to a woman unless you mean unconditional commitment to her and you are ready to be responsible and accountable for her spiritual condition. Young ladies, you should never believe that a man loves you unless he is ready to be committed to you unconditionally. Ladies, never tell a young man that you love him until he is ready to be a spiritual leader. Men, never believe that she loves you until she encourages you spiritually. I am not saying that you cannot be in love. Just do not arouse or awaken love until it so desires. Wait on God to bring you both to the same point, or risk destroying the potential for greatness.

So What Is Dating?

So, what is dating? There is no biblical precedent for dating because it does not exist in the Bible. We can look at relationships in the Bible and try to draw out principles, but there are no relationships in the Bible that model for us modern dating. That should be a sign that the way our culture does things may not be God's best for us. We can find other ways to accomplish the purpose of dating.

What is the purpose of dating? Well, there are two legitimate purposes for dating. We can date to build fellowship relationships with other believers, or we can date to find a mate (if we think we are ready for that). We can accomplish both of these purposes by going out in groups and by participating in structured activities at school, church, or in our community. When we hang out as friends, we should know the boundaries, and when we see someone has potential, we should know ourselves, be mindful of timing, and know the boundaries.

The problem is that we date for the wrong reasons. We date because our friends date or we are looking for love, security, or support. For some people, dating seems to be the only way to fill the void in their lives. We can see that all of these purposes fill some need that should be filled by our relationship with God. For some it is a way to assert our independence. For others it is just what we are expected to do. Whether we are breaking free from our parents or letting them (or others) decide who we are supposed to be, we cannot let dating determine our identity. We are to find our identity in our relationship with God as well. All of these purposes reveal a lack of maturity, spiritually and emotionally, to be in an exclusive relationship.

What is the big deal? There are very significant dangers related to the way we practice relationships in our culture. It should be obvious in the fact that so many marriages are falling apart, even among Christians, that the way we learn to have relationships is setting us up for failure. There are four main dangers that we face when we give into the cultural norm of dating.

The first danger is manipulation. Dating is often driven by wrong motives and causes us to perform and be something we are not. In even the best dating relationships, the game is being played, and that game is manipulation.

The second danger is isolation. When we enter into exclusive relationships, we tend to isolate ourselves from the network of people who supply our normal support and accountability. We spend less time with our family and friends, and no matter how hard we try, as we focus on our dating relationship we lose focus on our relationship with God.

The third danger breaks my heart more than any other. It is the danger of a trapped heart. When we enter into a dating relationship we give little parts of our self to the other person. We form an emotional bond that is deeper than can be defined by one of the appropriate, biblical love relationships. As we cross that boundary, an intimacy can develop that is only meant for the husband/wife relationship. If left unchecked, that intimacy will evolve into sex and then the war between our soul and our flesh begins. When that relationship ends, as most do, those pieces of yourself that you gave away are gone forever, and your heart is trapped in an emotional connection.

The final danger of dating is eternal loss. Yes, there are at least three things that you can lose for all of eternity by entering into a dating relationship.

The first is your heart. Like I just mentioned, when you give little pieces of your heart away, you can never get them back. If we practice this over and over, giving little pieces of ourselves away, our heart can become hard and the emotional scarring can cause permanent damage.

The second is your innocence. There is so much of adult life modeled in dating that can steal your innocence. When we open the door to what someone else might bring into the quiet places in our lives, we stand a good chance of losing those quiet places. As we are exposed to adult life, our childlike innocence is lost. That may seem like a good thing when you are fifteen, but it is an eternal loss that you will mourn the rest of your life.

The last thing is your virginity. We had to get around to it eventually. The fact is that virginity is a gift from God. It is a symbol of your purity that you can present to your mate as a pledge of your faithfulness. It is the seal of a covenant relationship with your spouse. If you give it away before it is time, it is eternally lost. God can forgive any sin, even sex, but once you have given your gift of virginity away it is an eternal loss. You have sealed your covenant with someone who is not your mate. God can make us new and give us a new start. However, we are not to tempt God by assuming His grace. The danger of dating is eternal loss.

If we are going to have integrity in our lives, then we must have it in our relationships. If we are going to have integrity in our relationships, then we must have a design for our relationships.

First, know the boundaries. We have established five biblical love relationships that are appropriate. We should be able to clearly define and measure all of our relationships by these five standards.

Second, have a purpose. What is the purpose of our relationships? Each of the five relationships has a clear purpose. We should know if the purpose of our relationship is witness, evangelism, fellowship, intimacy, or worship.

Third, establish standards. Based on the definition and purpose of our relationships, each one should have its own set of standards. Spiritual and emotional maturity implies the ability to establish and maintain standards in our relationships. These standards should always reflect the best that we can do, not the least that we can get away with. The who, what, when, and where of our relationships should all be established beforehand and should represent our best before God, not what we can get away with and still be viewed by others as a spiritual leader.

Finally, have a plan. In every relationship you have, establish in your mind what it will take to accomplish your purpose, within your boundaries, according to your standards, and then live accordingly. Remember, God desires for you to have wholeness in every area of your life, including your relationships.

CHAPTER 5

INSIGHT:
Seeing God's Will

You, however, did not come to know Christ that way. Surely you heard of him and were taught in him in accordance with the truth that is in Jesus. You were taught, with regard to your former way of life, to put off your old self, which is being corrupted by its deceitful desires; to be made new in the attitude of your minds; and to put on the new self, created to be like God in true righteousness and holiness. EPHESIANS 4:20–24

"Those who have most powerfully and permanently influenced their generation have been 'seers'— people who have seen more and farther than others —persons of faith, for faith is vision."
J. Oswald Sanders
Spiritual Leadership

As we work to establish in our lives an example of what a believer is supposed to be, to discipline ourselves to be godly, and to develop a wholeness in every area of our lives, we must be ever mindful of the goal that lies before us. As we work to put off the things of this world, we must understand that there must be a transformation of our minds before we can really begin to put on the things of God. That transformation of the mind is when we no longer think like a man or view the world like a man, but instead, we view the world like God views it and we have the mind of Christ.

What we are talking about here is insight. What we want to see here is what it means to have godly insight and how can we apply that to our lives in making everyday decisions. George Barna came out with research in 2003 where he interviewed teenagers from all over the country. Fifty-six percent of those teenagers said they attended church on a regular basis, but of those who participated in an active youth group, only fifty-three percent reported "understanding enough of the Bible so that every decision you make is based on biblical principles." Barna notes, "Less than one out of every ten churched teenagers has a biblical worldview. In other words, the result of their involvement at a church is that they can recite some religious facts, they made some friends, and they had fun. That's wonderful, but we also find that most of them have neither accepted Christ as their savior nor altered the basis on which they make their moral and ethical decisions in life."[4]

Insight, Vision, and Revelation

Insight is a deep understanding, a divine vision or revelation. It is a deep understanding of life from God's perspective. This definition tells us that there are two aspects to this deep understanding. First is divine vision. Vision is a sense of sight, apprehension or foresight. It is the ability to see, and what we mean here by a divine vision is a vision from God, a picture of what God has promised for your future. We often talk about this in terms of God's will or plan for your life.

---

[4] The Barna Group, Ltd., July 8, 2003, Teens Evaluate the Church-Based Ministry They Received as Children. From YouthPollSM, November 2002. Ventura, California. Need permission www.barna.org.

Second, seeing God's will is primarily about insight. I must say here that God's picture for your life is almost never about places and activities, but about who you are and about relationships. The Bible commands us to know God's will. It calls us to know God and become like Christ. In order to do that, we must have insight, a picture of what God has planned for our lives and a revelation.

A revelation is an act to disclose or manifest. It is the act of revealing something. A divine revelation is an act of God to disclose or manifest Himself. God has chosen to disclose who He is and how He works through His written word and to manifest Himself in the lives of believers around us, circumstances, and prayer. Jesus is the chief discloser and manifestation of God in this world, and all of what we know about Jesus is contained in Scripture. That is why our insight is dependant upon our relationship with God through the means by which he has chosen to reveal Himself, the Christ of Scripture.

Insight, as we talk about it here, is a picture of what God has planned for your life, based on our relationship with Him and His revelation of Himself to us. It is the combination of what we know about God and the picture that God has shown us of our lives, done so in a way that makes a real and practical difference in our lives. Insight is seeing life the way God sees it.

The Importance of Insight

Why is it important as leaders for us to have insight? John Maxwell says, "Vision is the indispensable quality of leadership." The ability to see ahead and chart a course for the future is a valuable quality in all leadership. However, spiritually speaking, it may be even more important than that. Henry Blackaby, in his book *Spiritual Leadership* shows us how.

> If Jesus provides the model for spiritual leadership, then the key is to obey and to preserve everything the Father reveals to [leaders] of His will. God has a vision of what He wants to do. He ask leaders to walk with Him so intimately that, when He reveals what is on His agenda, they will immediately adjust their lives to His will and the results will bring glory to God. This is not the model that many religious leaders, let alone business leaders, follow today, but it encompasses what biblical leadership is all about.[5]

God has a vision for our lives, a purpose and a plan. If we are going to fulfill His plan and become what He has created and called us to be, then we must have insight into that plan. God's visions for His people are impossible to achieve apart from insight into who God is and what He desires for us. John 5:19-20, 30 shows us that was true even for Christ Himself. *"I tell you the truth, the Son can do nothing by himself; he can do only what he sees his Father doing, because whatever the Father does the Son also does. For the Father loves the Son and shows him all he does. Yes, to your amazement he will show him even greater things than these. By myself I can do nothing; I judge only as I hear, and my judgment is just, for I seek not to please myself but him who sent me."*

Insight, vision and revelation, is essential to living the abundant, full life that God has planned for us and indispensable in leading others to that life by example. That is why when Helen Keller was asked what would be worse than being born blind, she responded, "The only thing worse than being born blind is to have sight without vision." She understood the value of not only seeing, but seeing what God wanted her to be.

---

[5]Blackaby, Henry, Spiritual Leadership.

How Do We Gain Insight?

Once we understand what insight is and why it is important to us as believers, and particularly as spiritual leaders, we can begin to investigate how we can gain insight. We have already seen that it is a gift from God that results from pursuing and receiving a vision from God through the revelation of God. These are supernatural events that are largely out of our control. All we can do is get into a place where we are ready to receive them and then ask. Fortunately, that is all that is required.

There are, however, some practical steps that we can take to put ourselves in a position to receive both a better picture of who God is and a picture of what God has planned for our future. It is not rocket science, and it has little to do with activity. Getting into a position to hear from God is all about attitude of the heart and relationship.

The first thing we have to do in order to be in a position to receive from God is to be renewed in our perspective. Romans 6:6 says, *"Knowing this, that our old self was crucified with Him, in order that our body of sin might be done away with, so that we would no longer be slaves to sin."* Insight means being renewed in your perspective, and being renewed in your perspective is all about putting off the old. The old self is trapped in the flesh and is represented by the things of this world. It is, as Ephesians 4 tells us, *"being corrupted by its deceitful desires."*

Most importantly, the old self offers us a perspective that is limited to the things of this world and lacks the ability to see from beyond the flesh. Therefore, we naturally see things from a human perspective. We see people from a human perspective and often judge their outward appearance or deeds. We see circumstances from a human perspective and allow them to suffocate us and cause us stress. We see God from a human perspective and we doubt that He is any more in control than we are. We make Him into our image instead of being made into His.

Perspective is all about position. If we are going to be in a position to receive from God, we have to get into a God position, a divine position. I am not saying that we become like gods or that we get in God's place. I am saying that we become like Christ and get where God is. Ephesians 1 tells us that God has every spiritual blessing stored up for us in heavenly places. What we have to do to access those blessings is get ourselves into heavenly places. One main way to do that is to be transformed in the way that we view things. We must learn to view things from a divine perspective. We see people the way God sees them and therefore see their souls and judge their hearts. We see circumstances from a divine perspective and allow them to work together for good. We see God the way He sees himself, and we begin to receive the revelation of who God really is. We are set free by the truth of who God is and we begin to be conformed to His image instead of Him being conformed, in our own minds, to ours.

My college pastor, Bro. Joe Guthrie, used to tell me that circumstances are like a mattress. If you lie underneath, you will suffocate. However, if you get on top, you can rest easy. Perspective is a matter of position and all about gaining God's vantage point. Time and space is like a number line, and our lives are played out among its points. When we look at life, we can see back five, maybe ten, points on the line. Some of us can see as far as two or three points into the future. However, insight is about seeing much more than that. God is above the line, looking down on the entire sheet of paper. He sees infinity past and infinity future all at once and understands every point on the line. We have to work to be transformed in our perspective so that we see things according to God's perspective and plan.

The fact that God knows everything—omniscience—is an overwhelming concept to us. However, I think it is less overwhelming than it should be. Omniscience means so much more than God knowing everything that happens to you. It even means more than the fact that He knows all that has happened and all that ever will happen. We have to understand that God knows everything. He knows not only what did happen but what could have happened. He knows not only what will happen, but what could happen. He has worked out all of the contingencies for your life and He has chosen the one that He knows will work out for the best, according to His purposes and for His glory. There is no need to doubt or second guess God's plan for your life. What we should try to do is to see things from His perspective. Then we will be free to be what God has called us to be.

The second thing we have to do in order to be in a position to receive from God is to be renewed in our vision. Romans 12:1–2 says, "*Therefore I urge you, brethren, by the mercies of God, to present your bodies a living and holy sacrifice, acceptable to God, which is your spiritual service of worship. And do not be conformed to this world, but be transformed by the renewing of your mind, so that you may prove what the will of God is, that which is good and acceptable and perfect.*" Insight means being renewed in your vision, and we have already seen that vision has to do with a picture of what God has planned for our lives. We are to be transformed in our minds, to have the spirit of our minds renewed, so that our thinking is transformed.

So often in the church we focus a great deal on putting off the old. We constantly tell students and new believers to stop this and stop that. We specialize in the long list of sins that represent the things of the world and our personal preferences, and we take on a pharisaical role of keeping the law. The ultimate end of this is legalism, and a great deal of our church life is centered around it.

Just as often, we focus more and more on putting on the new. We have an equally impressive list of things that the believer is supposed to do. We offer students and new believers all sorts of alternatives and give them an endless selection of new "spiritual things" to put on. We commercialize and mass produce Christianity, and we take on a marketing mentality in getting people "involved." The ultimate end of this is superficial spirituality, and a great deal of our church life is centered around it.

If we are ever truly going to put off the old and put on the new, we have to understand the key element is being transformed in the way we think. We have to discipline ourselves to be godly, to have the mind of Christ, and to think the way God thinks. Then we will begin to think about people the way God does. Instead of thinking about them in terms of what we can get out of them or from them, we will think of them in terms of how we can serve them. We will think with a grace mentality instead of deserving mentality. We will think about our life circumstances the way God thinks of them. We will view them as opportunities for God to reveal Himself in our lives and to teach, rather than simply opportunities to get ahead. We will rejoice in suffering rather than complain, and we will heal those who suffer instead of reject them. Insight is being renewed in the spirit of your mind, which in turn transforms your thinking.

It is a matter of seeing the picture. We must work to change the way we think, seeing the picture God has given us for our lives, seeing God's plan. If we strive to think like God thinks, we will see the picture that God has given us for our lives, not the picture we have drawn for ourselves or the picture the world (or the church) has drawn for us.

The third thing we have to do in order to be in a position to receive from God is to be renewed in our purpose. Rick Warren, with his book *The Purpose Driven Life*, has brought a lot of attention to the idea of purpose. It has affected so many people's lives because it is a key element to being in a position to receive from God. Ephesians 2:10 says, *"For we are His workmanship, created in Christ Jesus for good works, which God prepared beforehand so that we would walk in them."*

Insight means being renewed in your purpose, or changing the purpose of your life from a self-centered one to a divine-centered one. I have stated repeatedly that God has a plan for your life. What we need to understand is that plan has purpose behind it. God did not just develop a plan for your life in order to get you from one end to the other. He has a plan to prosper you, to do good works through you and to glorify Himself. God's plan has purpose, and we are to understand that His purpose for our lives is bigger and better than anything we could dream up for ourselves. Ephesians 3:20 tells us that God is, *"able to do far more abundantly beyond all that we ask or think, according to the power that works within us."*

The key to being renewed in our purpose is to begin to put on the new self, or take on the things of God. As I said before, putting on the new does not mean that we have to put on the latest Christian marketing fad. It does mean that we begin to take on the nature and character of God. We can only begin to see, think and act like God when we spend the majority of our time getting to know Him.

Transforming our purpose, putting on the new self or the things of God, is a matter of pursuit. I cannot see like Salvador Dali or Leonardo Da Vinci until I have studied their art. I cannot have vision like Abraham Lincoln or Ronald Reagan until I have studied their lives. I cannot think like Plato or Jonathan Edwards until I have read their writings and studied their logic. I cannot have godly insight unless I study God's word and work, who He is, what He has said. I cannot know what Jesus would do unless I know Him. I cannot know Him unless I pursue a relationship with Him.

God's purpose for each of our lives is particular and unique. What God has created and called me to be may be very different than what God has created and called you to be. We need to get used to that concept in the church. However, there are two things that are part of God's purpose and plan for every one of our lives:

Impact

God intends for us to be like Christ and for us to glorify Him with our lives. That is God's purpose or goal for each and every one of us. Insight is getting into a position to see that goal, seeing it in our individual lives, and then pursuing God's goal.

CHAPTER 6
IMITATION:
Walking in Christ

Therefore I, the prisoner of the Lord, implore you to walk in a manner worthy of the calling with which you have been called, with all humility and gentleness, with patience, showing tolerance for one another in love, being diligent to preserve the unity of the Spirit in the bond of peace. EPHESIANS 4:1–3

But whosoever would fully and feelingly understand the words of Christ, must endeavor to conform his life wholly to the life of Christ.
        Thomas a' Kempis
        The Imitation of Christ

As we seek not only to have temporal influence but to have a lasting impact on those around us for the cause of Christ, we need not only a picture of what God has for our future, but we need a guide. We need an example to follow ourselves. We need to know not only where we are going but how to get there from here. None of us would set out on a journey without some sort of guide. Though the days of good old maps may be gone, we can hardly get across town without our GPS or on-board navigational system. I personally depend a great deal on MapQuest and who does not love Google Earth. If we need a guide to get across town, across the state, or across the country, how much more do we need a guide for the most important adventure of our lives, our spiritual journey?

We have established Christ as the standard in our lives, and recognized the absolute necessity of having a wholeness in our lives that is faithful to the original. We have even gotten in a place to receive a picture from God of who He wants us to be and what He wants us to be about. All we need now is a map, a battle plan, a role-model. If our ultimate destination is to be like Christ, what better guide than Christ himself?

To Be an Imitator

Imitation, by definition, is the act or instance of imitating; something derived or copied from an original. It is reflecting the same nature and character as the original. Spiritually speaking, to be an imitator means to work to be like Christ in every way. Christ is the original, and He is already established in our lives as the standard by which we measure ourselves. Imitation is reflecting the nature and character of God in the reality of our daily lives.

Imitation, one of the primary forms of social learning, has been thought of as a low-level, animalistic phenomenon. However, work in the cognitive sciences has begun to show that it may be a rare and perhaps uniquely human ability, a gift from God that gives us a unique ability to live in the image of God.

> "There is a tendency to think of imitation as the "lowest" form of learning—"mere" imitation—and as having little place in the exalted reaches of adult and higher education. Nevertheless, Blackmore (1999)—whatever you think of the more specific claims of her thesis—has reclaimed it by demonstrating not only how

effective a form of learning imitation is, but also the sophistication required in order to be able to imitate.

Compared with the behavioral model of learning, which is a form of time-conflated evolution, imitation gets straight to the point. The teacher demonstrates or models, and the learner imitates. There are no "wrong" answers or dead ends: the quality of the learning is purely in the faithfulness of the reproduction of the action which has been demonstrated..."[6]

God, in His great wisdom, not only called us to be holy as He is holy, but He sent His Son to us as an example of what holiness is. Jesus told us that when we see Him we have seen the Father. His perfect submission to the will of the Father, His complete faithfulness to the original, is our model to follow. Our spiritual maturity is purely in our faithfulness to the person and work of Christ. His absolute obedience in the face of the same trials and temptations we suffer is a model for us to learn from and imitate.

The Importance of Imitation

We can see the inherent importance of imitation once we understand that it is a God-given means to living out the standard of Christ in our lives and being an example to others as we lead them toward where God wants them to be. However, there are at least three very particular things that our imitation of Christ accomplishes.

---

[6]Atherton, J S (2004), *Teaching and Learning: Imitation and social learning* [On-line] UK: Available: http://www.learningandteaching.info/learning/imitation.htm Accessed: 3 August 2005

The first thing that our imitation of Christ accomplishes is that it displays God's glory. 1 Corinthians 1:26–31 says;

> *Brothers, think of what you were when you were called. Not many of you were wise by human standards; not many were influential; not many were of noble birth. But God chose the foolish things of the world to shame the wise; God chose the weak things of the world to shame the strong. He chose the lowly things of this world and the despised things—and the things that are not—to nullify the things that are, so that no one may boast before him. It is because of him that you are in Christ Jesus, who has become for us wisdom from God—that is, our righteousness, holiness and redemption. Therefore, as it is written: "Let him who boasts boast in the Lord."*

When we imitate the nature and character of Christ, God is glorified because what He has done in our lives will be lifted up and not ourselves. Our foolishness will be turned to influence and nobility when we reflect Christ, because it will be turned into righteousness, holiness and redemption. We were created in the image of God to reflect His glory in His creation. Our sin tarnishes that reflection and prevents us from fulfilling our ultimate purpose in the universe. That is why the Bible characterizes sin as falling short of God's glory. Once our sin has been removed by the work of Christ and it has been replaced by His righteousness, our entire lives become a living, sacrificial act of submission and obedience, for the glory of God. Through our imitation of Christ, our foolishness becomes for us wisdom from God. When we imitate Christ, we boast in the Lord.

The second thing that our imitation of Christ accomplishes is that it reveals Christ to others. When we imitate the nature and character of Christ in our lives, we will be able to say as Paul says in 1 Corinthians 1:11, "*Follow my example, as I follow the example of Christ.*" In Ephesians 5:1-2, Paul gives us a clear command and explanation of how our imitation of Christ will reveal Christ to others. "*Be imitators of God, therefore, as dearly loved children and live a life of love, just as Christ loved us and gave himself up for us as a fragrant offering and sacrifice to God.*" This is a clear command to be imitators of Christ. We do that by living a life of love. Jesus told us that it was by our love for one another that the world would know that we are God's children. It is by imitating the love of God that Christ will be revealed to others. It is because of God's great love for us that He sent Jesus to die for our sins, and because of Jesus' great love for the Father that He was willing to submit His will to that of the Father's and obey to the point of death, even death on a cross. When we imitate Christ with our lives, others will see the nature and character of Christ in us. They will be drawn to Him through the revelation of His character in our lives. It is only by imitating that sacrificial love that our lives will reflect Christ to a lost world.

The third thing that our imitation of Christ accomplishes is that it reveals God's will to us. This may seem like a bold statement. However, Romans 12:1-2 very clearly connects the imitation of Christ to seeing God's will. "*Therefore, I urge you, brothers, in view of God's mercy, to offer your bodies as living sacrifices, holy and pleasing to God—this is your spiritual act of worship. Do not conform any longer to the pattern of this world, but be transformed by the renewing of your mind. Then you will be able to test and approve what God's will is—his good, pleasing and perfect will.*"

Our imitation of the sacrificial love of Christ will call us to offer up our own lives as living sacrifices before God. Our imitation of Christ will be holy and pleasing to God, it will be a spiritual act of worship before God, and if we transform our way of thinking and imitate that mind of Christ, God's will is not only revealed to us, but this verse clearly says that we will experience it, testing it to see that it is good, pleasing and perfect.

Imitation allows us to not only know the will of God in an intellectual sense or to see it in a spiritual sense. Imitation allows us to experience the will of God. We will walk in the will of God, as Christ walked in the will of God, as we imitate Christ in every area. We will test God's will and find it just as Christ found it. It will prove itself to be sufficient. It will prove to be positive, rewarding and uniquely suited for us.

Walking in Christ

So, how do we do it? How do we walk in manner worthy of the calling by which we have been called? How do we imitate the nature and character of the life of Christ in our lives and reflect it to a watching world? We have to remember that God is not so much concerned about activity as He is the integrity of our hearts, the wholeness of our devotion to Him, our delight in the things of God, and the sacrifice of our lives to Him. As a life lived in a manner worthy of our calling will bear the particular fruit of humility, gentleness, and patience, showing tolerance and preserving unity, the elements of that life are much the same: that we live consistently in a manner that shows absolute fidelity to the standard of Christ and a desire to become just like Him.

The first thing that imitation involves is consistency. As leaders and examples, we have to understand that what people are looking for is not just an example, but a consistent example. A walk is a long progression in a determined direction. What that means is that our example should, over the long term, lead in one consistent direction.

The Bible often characterizes our journey to spiritual maturity as a walk. That is to imply that it is directional. When we were dead in our sins, we were walking in the bondage of sin, toward sin, death and hell. God cried out in eternity and said, "I love you." That gracious call of God stopped us in our tracks and compelled us to respond, "What shall I do to be saved?" God responds, "NOTHING." He said that faith is the key. "Simply trust that I am who I say I am and can do what I say I can do." You must demonstrate that faith by believing in your heart that Jesus is Lord and confessing with your mouth that God raised Him from the dead.

Once we, by faith, receive God's merciful gift of grace, we are called to repent, or turn away from our sin and turn toward Christ. Where we were once walking toward sin, death and hell, we are now facing Christ's righteousness, salvation and eternal fellowship with God. Our calling from that moment is to walk: walk in righteousness, walk in salvation. We are to walk toward righteousness, abundant and eternal life, and perfect fellowship with the Father in heaven. In our walk, we are to be imitators of Christ, to walk in a manner worthy of our calling.

We have already seen that integrity is of great importance and that our talk should match our walk and our walk should match the reality of our hearts. However, so many times, we as believers get so caught up in the individual steps of the Christian life that we lose track of where it is we are going or why we started on this pilgrimage in the first place. That over-emphasis on the individual step is legalism, and much of our religious life is caught up in it. We are to obey the commands of God, but we cannot move from where we are to where God wants us to be if we are looking to the law or the preferences of man instead of to Christ. The whole point of the law is to show that we need a savior. People cannot follow us from where they are to where God wants them to be if we are aware only of the steps and blind to the destination. We have to be able to look ahead and talk about where we are going and why.

Christ came to set us free, and Scripture proclaims that the Truth will set you free. Therefore, we are free indeed. We have great liberty as believers because we are free from the bondage of sin, and grace provides an emancipation from the boundaries of this world. However, we must understand that we are still at war with the flesh and the world. We must be mindful of how we walk. Paul makes clear that while nothing is illegal for us, some things are not profitable. We have to understand that we cannot walk around with our heads in the clouds without being mindful of our steps. We must be disciplined and train ourselves to be godly. We must pay attention to our steps, or we will just be out on a meandering stroll and we will be no example. The over-emphasis on the freedom to walk is liberalism, and much of our secular life is built upon it. So much of our culture is built on the abstract nature of things. We live in a generation of undefined truth and relativism. Tolerance and randomness are often seen as the highest virtues. However, people will not follow if you are just wandering around going in no particular direction at all. Have you ever driven behind an elderly couple out on a Sunday afternoon drive?

All things prove themselves over time, and that is why we cannot measure our spiritual walk by a single day or event. A spiritual walk is defined by the rightness of each step, but only as much as it leads in a particular direction. We are all going to mess up and get off course from time to time. Sometimes it is trying too hard to stay on course that makes us lose our way. We are to walk in a balanced way that keeps both the trees and the forest in view. We must be mindful of both our steps and our direction so that those who follow us know both how and where to walk.

The second thing that imitation involves is fidelity to the original. To walk in a manner worthy of the calling by which you have been called or of the gospel does not mean that you become worthy of it or have earned it. What it does mean is that you reflect the same nature and character as the One who called you.

When thinking about this concept, I am always reminded of when I was little and my brothers and I would go to the grocery store with our mother. We are from the generation of grocery-store feet, while our children are from the generation of Germ-X. Before she would let us get out of the car, she would always give us the same speech. "Now you boys remember how to act in here. Don't go in here and make fools out of yourselves. You will not only embarrass yourselves but also your dad and me." How we acted in public reflected on my parents somehow, and I never really understood that until I got out on my own.

When I started going to the grocery store as an adult, I would see little children running up and down aisles, pitching a fit in the floor, or begging their parents for some chocolate-based cereal with a toy. My immediate reaction was, "Who are that kid's parents?" No matter how hard I tried to stop it, I always thought, "Where are his parents and why don't they do something with him?" No matter how hard I fought, I always felt, "What kind of parent lets their kid get away with stuff like that?" Now it is obvious that I did not have children of my own then, and now that I do I understand where those parents were and why they didn't do something. It takes a great deal of patience to train your children in the way they should go in the grocery store. You have to do a lot of work before you get there, and I guess that is what my mom was trying to do. Let's face it, no one wants to be that kid's parent.

The point is that when others see us out in public, the way we act reflects on our parents and people assume that we are reflecting the character of our parents in our behavior. The same thing is true at a much deeper level for us spiritually. God is not so much concerned with what is on the outside, but He is intensely concerned about how our behavior reflects on His nature and character. It is God's intention that when others see us walking out in the world they say, "There goes one of God's children. He looks just like Him, talks just like Him and acts just like Him." Our walk is to have a particular character to it, because the One who calls us has a particular character. We are to walk in a manner that reflects fidelity to the original: humility, gentleness, patience, love, unity. People can and will follow an example like that.

The third thing that imitation involves is a particular result. A walk that reflects the nature and character of God will have purpose to it. Again, we will not just be out for a walk in the woods with no particular destination. What kind of leaders would we be if a bunch of people were following us to nowhere? A leader has vision and purpose, and one of the essential elements of leadership is that a leader leads to a particular place or outcome. Henry Blackaby says, "Spiritual leadership is leading people from where they are to where God wants them to be." Robert Clinton, in his book *The Making of a Leader*, says, "The central task of a spiritual leader is influencing God's people toward God's purposes."[7] Our walk should not only have a particular character to it, but also a particular outcome, because the One who calls us has a particular purpose in calling us. His purpose is that we should be like Christ and glorify Him with our lives.

Once we have turned from sin, death and hell and begun to walk in righteousness, life and eternity, we must keep those goals in view. When Paul says in Philippians 3, *"One thing I do: forgetting what lies behind and straining forward to what lies ahead, I press on toward the goal for the prize of the upward call of God in Christ Jesus,"* he is giving us a picture of the result of our walk. We are walking toward the goal, to receive the upward call of God. The prize is the resurrection, the moment we become complete, when we are finally conformed to the image of Christ in glorification. Therefore, the particular outcome of our walk is Christ-likeness.

Christ-likeness is being conformed to the likeness of Christ, or becoming a look-a-like, an imitator. God's calling for you is to be a fully mature image of Christ. You have permission to be just

---

[7]Blackaby, Henry T. and Richard, Spiritual Leadership, pg. 17, 20; Broadman & Holman Publishers, Nashville, TN: 2001.

like Christ. We have been taught for so long to view ourselves as sinners and to promote our own false humility. We are sinners saved by grace. But what does grace do in our lives if we still view ourselves as sinners? That gives us excuse to fail and creates an expectation that we will fall short.

We may well fall short. In fact all have and all do, and we must never underestimate the power of our sinful flesh and the temptation of this world. However, when we were set free from sin by Christ's work on the cross, we were made free indeed. Sin now no longer has a hold on us and we are no longer obliged by the old nature to sin. If we sin as a new creation, it is because we choose to neglect our saintly position and decide to accept less than God's best. In fact, true humility is more in recognizing our victory in Christ, depending on Him for all things, and viewing Him as all sufficient, not in admitting defeat and expecting failure. Not only do you have permission from God, but it is one of God's basic purposes in the universe that you be just like Christ.

God is faithful to complete that which He has begun, and He is now in the process of making us like Christ. That should not only be our goal, our future, but our current state. Once again, you can never be in the future what you are not becoming today. That is why the Christian life is not about doing the least you can get by with and still be considered a good Christian, but instead about what is the best that you can do to be like Christ in your life. We are more than conquerors. We are children of the King, princes and princesses, saints of the most High God. So, as we walk, we ought to have a goal in view. That goal is Christ-likeness—to be so much like Christ, conformed to His likeness and transformed into His image, that when the Father calls us home it is but a small step from this life to the next. It is not about the least you can get away with but the best that you can do. And you have permission from God to be just like Christ. In fact, it is promised.

For God is not unjust so as to forget your work and the love which you have shown toward His name, in having ministered and in still ministering to the saints. And we desire that each one of you show the same diligence so as to realize the full assurance of hope until the end, so that you will not be sluggish, but imitators of those who through faith and patience inherit the promises. HEBREWS 6:10–12

CHAPTER 7
INTENSITY:
Counting the Costs

Finally brothers, be strong in the Lord and in the power of His might. Put on the full armor of God, that you might be able to stand against the schemes of the devil. For we do not wrestle against flesh and blood, but against principalities and powers, against the rulers of the darkness of this age, against spiritual hosts of wickedness in the heavenly places. EPHESIANS 6:10–12

The reward belongs to the man who is actually in the arena: whose face is marred by dust and sweat and blood; who strives valiantly; who errs and comes up short again and again; who knows in the end the triumph of high achievement; and who, at worst, if he fails, at least he fails while daring greatly, so that his place shall never be with those cold timid souls who know neither victory nor defeat.
    Theodore Roosevelt, 20th Century

As the great quote from President Roosevlet reminds us, leadership is about so much more than integrity, vision and conviction. Leadership is about understanding the reality of circumstances and having the passion and intensity to face that reality head

Impact   87

on. Courage is one of the most essential attributes of a maturing believer. However, this is not a typical courage that knows no fear, but a spiritual courage that acknowledges the danger of spiritual warfare and moves ahead by faith. The essential element here is not supernatural bravery, but trust in the supernatural power of God. Spiritual courage does not stand in oppostiion to humilty, but grows out of it as part of our dependence on God. We must understand that living a life of impact means that we have to count the cost. Along the way there will be many battles to fight and we must choose those battles wisely. We must also recognize when we reach a hill on which to die. On those hills we are charged to stand firm. We must stand in the intesity of war. That intensity requires a spiritual power, a spiritual preparation and a divine plan fit for spiritual battles.

The Power of Intensity

It is obvious that being a real spiritual leader is not a job for the faint of heart. Though it is a calling every one of us has on our lives, we will certainly fulfill that calling at different levels. Some of us may simply have greater influence because of our social status, athletic ability, personality, or platform. Some people are better able to turn that influence into lasting impact because they have come to a deeper place of integrity, insight, or imitation in their walk. However, all of these factors only go so far if we do not understand that what we are involved in is a spiritual war. If we have influence, integrity, insight, and imitation but fail to live with intensity in our hearts, we will fail to reach our full potential as examples of those who believe, because we do not have the sense of urgency that is always necessary for greatness.

So, what is intensity? Intensity is defined as the state of being intense to an extreme degree, as in intensity of heat, cold, mental application, or passion. However, there is more to intensity than being extreme. Intensity is literally the amount or degree of energy with which a force operates or a cause acts; effectiveness, as estimated by results produced. We are a force for the cause of Christ in this spiritual battle that rages in the universe. Intensity is the energy with which we operate or act on behalf of that cause, and our intensity is measured not by how extreme we may or may not be, but by the results produced. Like our battle, the fruits are not always physical and measurable by men. In this battle, the magnitude of disturbed force, such as pressure, stress, or weight, produces perseverance and spiritual maturity.

I think of that great battle scene at the beginning of the movie *Gladiator*. We know the basic story line and we can see the respect that the Roman legion has for Maximus. We will soon learn of his courage, conviction, and perseverance, and we understand he is a great leader as we watch him lead his men into battle. However, in those smoky moments before the conflict, there is only one thing that allows us to feel the weight of the moment. It is the intensity of battle that fills every movement and every word. Intensity is the final ingredient and it is all about preparation.

The Preparation of Intensity

Preparing for battle must be one of the most intense moments that a human being can experience. Fortunately, most of us will never have to experience that at a human level. I can only relate it to my experiences of having been in the locker room before a big game. I remember well the intensity of getting ready to go out and play. The potential for greatness lay before you while defeat lurked in the next room. There you are, preparing to meet your moment. Everything is at stake and yet you seem to have nothing to lose. I can only imagine that there is a similar sense for soldiers who are preparing to enter battle. Years of preparation have gone into this moment, and though death itself may sit at the door, so does the opportunity to fight for a cause larger than yourself. The people around you, your country—freedom itself—loom as motivators to fight sacrificially. To live is Christ and to die is gain because there is no greater demonstration of love than for a man give himself up for another. There is a mysterious truth to what Jesus says in Matthew 16:25: *"For whoever wishes to save his life will lose it; but whoever loses his life for My sake will find it."*

Again, a hundred scenes from a dozen movies come to mind that would illustrate the intensity of preparation that we are talking about. However, Paul gives us a great description of the preparation that having a sense of urgency that comes with intensity requires when he tells us in Ephesians 6:13–18, *"Take up the full armor of God, so that you will be able to resist in the evil day, and having done everything, to stand firm."*

It seems such an easy calling to simply stand firm. At least it sounds easy enough. No battle call, no charge of the Light Brigade. Just stand. It does not sound like much of a battle or much of an adventure. The truth is, just standing around waiting for something to happen does not sound very exciting at all. That is, until we add the intensity of battle. Take up your armor! The battle is at hand and we are to suit up. But why, where is the battle? Oh, don't you feel the silence all around you? Put on your armor so that you will be ready when the day of evil arrives! You must prepare now so that you will be able to resist, to fight, when your moment of greatness arrives. Put on your armor, and having done everything you know to do to be ready, stand firm!

Intensity makes all of the difference, and it comes from understanding the circumstances and consequences. It comes from counting the costs of battle, and it gives us a sense of urgency that helps us to prepare to stand firm.

So what is our preparation? First, it is to take up the full armor of God. We are called to get dressed for battle. Because our battle is spiritual, our armor must also be spiritual. Therefore, we do not just put on any old armor, but the armor of the living God. If we are wise, we will not just put on parts, selecting what is comfortable for us to wear or what we naturally look good in. If we are going to stand in the day of evil, we must put it all on.

First, we must wear truth around our waist as a foundation for all the other armor of God, for every other attribute and action of God is based on His truth. If God were not true, every other thing about God would be called into question and He would not be God. Truth, like a belt, holds us together. Therefore, when we hear this word "truth," let us understand that Paul means here a wholeness that excludes all hypocrisy. He refers to an integrity that would have us go to battle for God with an open heart, not with eye service, not as before men, but with pure, humble and selfless intentions.

Second and connected to truth, is righteousness. Of course, we know we have no righteousness of our own. So, we wear the righteousness of Christ as a breastplate. It covers our heart and vital organs and makes us fearless in battle, for we know that if we take the armor God gives us, we will be sure to have victory over our enemies. With our identity in Christ covering the depth of our being, we stand steadfast, upright, and without fraud or malice. We can stand with our chest out, for no matter our enemy or the perceptions of men, we wear our right standing before God on our chest.

Third, after securing the core of our being with integrity and holiness, we are called to put on boots. Paul gives the gospel the power to shoe us, protecting our feet and making us able to stand, as we are trained in it. That is why our boots are not the gospel itself, but the preparation of the gospel. We must stand in the preparation of the gospel. We must be wholly immersed in it and receive the instruction from it. And what is it that we receive from the gospel? That we who were once enemies of God are now made His own possession. That is why Paul adds to the title of the gospel, *"the gospel of peace."*

And by this gives us courage to fight, as if he should say, My friends, it is true that your enemies are mighty and will give you dreadful alarms, insomuch that you would not be able to withstand them without being overthrown a hundred thousand times in an hour, if God did not aid you. But if you do not despise the succor (help in need) God gives you, but rather prove its worth by striving to withstand all evil, you will have peace in the midst of war. And why? Because the gospel always brings that benefit with it.[8]

Fourth, in addition to all, having done everything, we are to take up the shield of faith. Faith is a belief or confidence, and it is our confidence in God that allows us to stand against our enemy. As we stand firm, we understand that we are under attack. Confidence in the nature and character of God produces perseverance in us as we are attacked, and we know that perseverance produces character, and character hope. To hope is to live and to live means to continue to stand. Faith is our shield, the protection from attack that allows us to withstand the attack of the enemy and to remain standing after the fight is done.

The Romans had a long, rectangular shield that guarded them from their chin to their knees. This shield was heavy and was in no way easy to carry. However, it was essential for protecting the soldier from the spears and arrows of the enemy. It would be made of wood but covered with cloth and leather so that the soldiers could soak their shields in water. The water-soaked shield would extinguish the fiery arrows of the enemy.

---

[8]Calvin, John, *Sermons on The Epistle to the Ephesians,* Banner of Truth, Carlisle, Pennsylvania, 1987; p.671.

It is the believer's faith, or trust in God, that is above all necessary to protect him from the frontal attack of the enemy. Temptation is most often likened to the fiery darts of the enemy, and it burns us when it is not quenched. It is the shield of faith that allows us to stand against temptation without being burned by it. But only when our shield has been soaked in the living water is it useful to put out the fire of temptation. It is not a measure of faith that is important, but the object or quality of faith that serves to protect.

Fifth, we are to take the helmet of salvation. Now the head is obviously a major target in any form of battle. This is not only true in the physical sense, but also in the figurative sense. Our mind is the only place Satan can attack our salvation. Paul is speaking to the believer here. Therefore, he is clearly not talking about attaining salvation. He is talking about salvation as the means of protection for our mind. Satan's goal is to cause us to live outside of our salvation. The best way he can accomplish this is to cause us to doubt our salvation or to continue to think in ways that do not reflect the fact that we are saved. He uses the weapons of doubt, discouragement, confusion, and fear to injure our spiritual minds. He uses them to rob us of the mind of Christ and therefore cause us not to be transformed by the renewing of our minds, but instead to be conformed to the pattern of this world. Then, our testimony is hindered, our witness is diluted, and we struggle to exist rather than living an eternal and abundant life because we do not test and prove the good, pleasing, and perfect will of God.

It is the helmet of the assurance of our salvation that guards our minds from this deceitful attack. Satan knows that he cannot attack the salvation of a true believer. Therefore, he uses subtle weapons to cause us to doubt our salvation. Our security in Christ is the fact in which God would have us to live and which will guard our minds. We can be secure because our salvation does not depend on our own works of merit or righteousness, but only on the grace of God. The assurance that results from this fact serves as a protection for our divine perspective, vision, and purpose.

The final piece of armor that Paul urges us to take up as part of our preparation is the sword of the Spirit. Finally, a weapon! The only weapon we need in preparation to stand firm is the Word of God. God's Word is more powerful than any of Satan's darts, arrows or spears. The sword is used both to fend off the attacks of Satan, as Jesus did when tempted in the desert, and to destroy the strategies of the enemy, as Jesus does in Matthew 21 when He cleansed the Temple.

However, I believe the most effective work of the Word of God in our preparation for battle is the work it does in us. The Bible tells us in Hebrews 4:12, *"The word of God is living and active and sharper than any two-edged sword, and piercing as far as the division of soul and spirit, of both joints and marrow, and able to judge the thoughts and intentions of the heart."* The Sword of the Spirit does its primary work in piercing us. It prepares us for battle by judging the intentions of our hearts. In that way, it is an invaluable part of our defense against the stealth attacks of Satan called selfishness and pride. However, a sword is only useful if you take it up. A sword left on the shelf is neither defense nor weapon.

So that you will be able to resist in the evil day, so that you will be able to stand firm, stand and take up the full armor of God: belt, breastplate, boots, shield, helmet and sword. Pray in the Spirit on all occasions with all kinds of prayers and requests. With this in mind, be alert and always keep on praying for all the saints. Remember, it is all about relationship, not activity. The armor all comes from our relationship with God through Christ and is rendered useless apart from that relationship. We are to fellowship with God always, thanking God and asking God for all things.

Our prayer lives are to be "in the Spirit" and therefore in line with the will of God. The attitude of our prayer lives should be "watchful" that we are in line with the will of God and "watchful" because our enemy is prowling around us. So, we should persevere in our prayers and request for all saints, that they would have intensity and be prepared for the battle that comes.

The Plan of Intensity

Putting on the armor is only half the preparation for battle. There is much more to getting ready to play a football game than putting on pants, shoulder pads, cleats, and a helmet. If you are going to be successful, you must know who you are playing against and have a game plan for defeating them. In order to be ready to fight in this spiritual battle, we must know our enemy and understand what we must do to defeat him.

Know your enemy. Our enemy is clearly defined for us in Scripture. Here, Paul refers to him as the devil, and on his team are principalities and powers, rulers of the darkness of this age, and spiritual hosts of wickedness. It would be a formidable team if we were to face them alone. However, their power is limited, their schemes are ancient, and the defeat is certain. If we stand firm in Christ, we will have victory.

The coach of the opposing team is the devil, and we are to stand against his schemes. So, who is he and what are his schemes? 1 Peter 5:8–9 tells us that he is a prowling lion and his scheme is to devour us. *"Be self-controlled and alert. Your enemy the devil prowls around like a roaring lion looking for someone to devour. Resist him, standing firm in the faith, because you know that your brothers throughout the world are undergoing the same kind of sufferings."*

The verse does not say that he is a roaring lion. It says that he is like a roaring lion in that he prowls around looking for someone to devour. He is no courageous lion, roaring as he comes. He is a coward who prowls around in the shadows and dark places. True courage comes from God. Courage comes from being truly free. Satan is a coward who simply acts like a prowling lion. However, the reality is that he seeks for someone to devour. The cowardly lion cannot devour the mighty soldier of God. He looks for someone weak and wounded to devour. Therefore, we are simply to stand firm, be self-controlled, and be alert. If we are paying attention and do not open doors for him to enter into our lives by our lack of discipline, we will be able to resist him and stand firm. Execute, no penalties and no turnovers. Our opponent hangs around and looks for a chance to take advantage. If we play it smart, Christ's victory will be made complete in us.

In John 10:10 we are given another helpful picture of our opponent. There, Jesus tells us that the devil is a thief and his scheme is to steal, kill, and destroy. *"The thief comes only to steal and kill and destroy; I came that they may have life, and have it abundantly."*

Again, our opponent does not boldly stand before us and accept our challenge to fight like the brave Germanic warriors in *Gladiator*. He is rather characterized as a thief. He sneaks around and looks for a way in, waiting until we are asleep or our guard is down. He waits in the shadows until we take our armor off and then comes at us under cover of night, or he waits until we leave our house unguarded and finds a window left open or door unlocked. Again, he is a coward, a sorry thief and criminal, but the reality is that he seeks to steal, kill and destroy.

The thief comes only to steal. He comes to steal life. The metaphor here is one of Jesus being the good shepherd who watches over His sheep. Those who enter by any other way than by His gate are thieves and robbers. Therefore, those under the protection of the shepherd are His sheep who hear His voice and come to Him. He is talking about believers. Therefore, we know that He is not talking about the thief being able to steal salvation, or the life of Christ itself. What the thief steals is the joy of the life of Christ. He comes in over the fence to steal our joy of living away from us. If he can cause us to not delight in the Lord, then he has robbed us of a true understanding of what it means to serve God and of a true testimony to the greatness of God.

The thief comes only to kill. Again, He cannot end the life of Christ in us. What the thief comes to kill is the abundant life we have in Christ. He comes in over the fence to cause us to cease to live abundantly. If he can cause us to simply exist, without passion or purpose, then he has killed our spirit and made us complacent, possibly even apathetic, believers, dead and useless tools in the hands of a master. He has made us like branches that bear no fruit. We are as dead, dried and withered. We cease to live in the supernatural and therefore our lives have no power before men.

The thief comes only to destroy. He cannot take eternal and abundant life away from us, but he can come to destroy it. He comes over the fence and causes our lives to be blown apart. He can destroy our influence and our impact by destroying our integrity or our intensity. He cannot remove the gift of life. When he cannot steal the joy of life or kill the abundance of life, he will try to destroy the fruit of life. He comes to bring nothing because he has nothing, and if he can't have it he is determined that no one will. While Satan came to kill, steal and destroy, Jesus came that we might have life and have it to the full.

Know the plan. Now that we understand our adversary, what he is attempting to do in our lives and why, we can begin to look to our example for a battle plan for confronting our enemy. Jesus came face to face with our enemy in the desert, and there He gave us a game plan to overcome the devil and his ancient schemes.

Immediately after coming out of the baptismal waters and receiving the praise of God as His "beloved Son, in whom I am well pleased," The Bible tells us that Jesus was led by the Holy Spirit into the desert for the express purpose of being tempted by the enemy.

Jesus fasted for forty days and forty nights. Luke tells us that He was tempted for the full forty days of His fast. At the end of these days, Jesus was hungry, and Satan came to Him. Satan came with three specific temptations; "*If you are the Son of God, command this stone to become bread,*" "*If you will worship before me all will be yours,*" and "*If you are the Son of God, throw yourself down from here and let the angels protect you.*"

There is no doubt that Satan believed that Jesus is the Son of God or he would not have tempted Him in this way. There is no doubt Jesus believed that He was the Son of God or He would not have been tempted by Satan's claims at all. The tempting by Satan was threefold; the lust of the flesh, the lust of the eye, and the pride of life. It is a simple scheme that is old as man himself.

In Genesis 3, Satan came to tempt man in the Garden of Eden, and we find his schemes the same then as when he confronted Jesus. The enemy is described here as deceitful, and so he goes after the woman, who had received her instruction from Adam, not God, and was therefore more vulnerable to his attack. The point is, he is a liar and a coward. He began to question what God had said to Adam, and in turn caused Eve to question what Adam had taught her. After the snake convinced her that the law God had given Adam could be interpreted liberally, he said to her, "*You will not surely die. For God knows that in the day that you eat of it your eyes will be opened, and you will be like God, knowing good and evil.*" This is the same temptation with which he tempted Jesus—that you can be in control and you can be a god unto yourself. Having had her eyes opened to this possibility, Eve then views the fruit differently. "*So then the woman saw that the tree was good for food,*" the lust of the flesh, "*that it was pleasant to the eye,*" the lust of the eye, "*and a tree desirable to make one wise,*" the pride of life, "*she took of its fruit and ate it.*" His schemes are as ancient as the most ancient of days.

Here is how Jesus overcame these schemes. Satan did not tempt Jesus with being filled, with power and authority, or with heavenly protection. He had all of that. Satan tempted Jesus to circumvent the plan of God, to take matters into His own hands, and become God unto Himself, just like he had done with Adam and Eve. It was Jesus' relationship with the Father that Satan was after, because all of Jesus' greatness was wrapped up in His connection to the Father.

Jesus was wise to Satan's ancient schemes. He attacked him with the sword of the Spirit, showing first that He was dependant on God for His provision, like Israel in the desert. *"Man shall not live by bread alone, but by every word of God."* Second, Jesus showed that He reserved the place of worship in His life for only one person, God the Father. *"You shall worship the Lord your God, and Him only you shall serve."* Third, Jesus showed that God was the giver and taker of life and that as such, He was not to be messed with. *"You shall not tempt the Lord your God."* Even Satan quoted Scripture in verse 10 of Luke's account, but it was empty and full of deceit. So how was it that Jesus' words caused Satan to be defeated and flee? The sword had great effect when wielded by Jesus because He was shielded by truth, righteousness, peace, faith, and eternal security. It was His wholeness, vision, and fidelity to the original that gave Him influence unto victory. It is submission to the will of the Father that brought victory both here and in the Garden of Gethsemane, when Jesus finally cried, *"Not my will but Yours be done."*

The defeat of our enemy is sure because of the victory of Jesus both in the desert and on the cross. That defeat is pictured for us in Revelation 20.

> *Then I saw an angel coming down from heaven, holding the key of the abyss and a great chain in his hand. And he laid hold of the dragon, the serpent of old, who is the devil and Satan, and bound him for a thousand years; and he threw him into the abyss, and shut it and sealed it over him, so that he would not*

> deceive the nations any longer, until the thousand years were completed; after these things he must be released for a short time.
>
> When the thousand years are completed, Satan will be released from his prison, and will come out to deceive the nations which are in the four corners of the earth, Gog and Magog, to gather them together for the war; the number of them is like the sand of the seashore. And they came up on the broad plain of the earth and surrounded the camp of the saints and the beloved city, and fire came down from heaven and devoured them. And the devil who deceived them was thrown into the lake of fire and brimstone, where the beast and the false prophet are also; and they will be tormented day and night forever and ever. REVELATION 20:1–3, 7–10

That defeat is shown to be made sure for us in 1 John 2:14, "*I have written to you, fathers, because you know Him who has been from the beginning I have written to you, young men, because you are strong, and the word of God abides in you, and you have overcome the evil one.*" It is also shown to be coming quickly for us in Romans 16:19–20, "*For the report of your obedience has reached to all; therefore I am rejoicing over you, but I want you to be wise in what is good and innocent in what is evil. The God of peace will soon crush Satan under your feet the grace of our Lord Jesus be with you.*" We can easily see that for that result to be made complete in us, we must be obedient to the will of God. Interestingly, the result is quite the opposite of what Satan promised Eve, "*to be wise in what is good and innocent in what is evil.*"

LEGACY

Jonathan Edwards (1703–1758) was a theologian and preacher who was instrumental in forming the character of colonial American life. His overall contribution places him as one of the greatest theologians ever and as a top colonial figure. During his twenty-three years as a pastor in Northampton, Massachusetts, he saw true revival in 1734–1735 and again in The Great Awakening of 1740. In 1741, Edwards delivered possibly the most famous sermon ever written, "Sinners in the Hands of an Angry God". Edwards went on to lead the Native American Mission in Stockbridge, Massachusetts, where he wrote four great philosophical and theological works. He later became the President of Princeton College. Before dying of a smallpox vaccination, he and Sarah, his wife of thirty-one years, had eleven children.[9]

In 1900, A.E. Winship studied what happened to the 1,400 descendants of Jonathan and Sarah by the year 1900. He found they included 13 college presidents, 65 professors, 100 lawyers and a dean of a law school, 30 judges, 66 physicians and a dean of a medical school, and 80 holders of public office, including three U.S. Senators, mayors of three large cities, governors of three states, a Vice-President of the United States, and a controller of

---

[9]"Jonathan Edwards," *Concise Dictionary of Christianity in America*, InterVarsity Press, Downers Grove, Illinois, 1995.

the United States Treasury. Collectively they had written over 135 books and edited 18 journals and periodicals. Many had entered the ministry. Over 100 were missionaries, and others were on mission boards.[10]

The following is a letter Edwards wrote to his eldest son Timothy, who at age fourteen, while on a trip to New York and New Jersey, had been exposed to small-pox. While in New York, he fell ill with fever. The letter shows not only Edwards' love and care but his understanding that our chief concern should always be for the spiritual condition, because if we are going to leave a lasting legacy, it must necessarily be by the cause of God.

> Stockbridge, April 1753
>
> My Dear Child,
>
> Before you will receive this letter, the matter will doubtless be determined, as to your having the small-pox. You will either be sick with that distemper, or will be past danger of having it, from any infection taken in your voyage. But whether you are sick or well, like to die or like to live, I hope you are earnestly seeking your salvation. I am sure there is a great deal of reason it should be so, considering the warnings you have had in word and in providence. That which you met with, in your passage from New York to Newark, which was the occasion of your fever, was indeed a remarkable warning, a dispensation full of instruction, and a very loud call of God to you to make haste, and do not delay in the great business of religion.

---

[10] "Jonathan Edwards: America's Humble Giant," Christian History Institute, http://chi.gospelcom.net/GLIMPSEF/Glimpses/glmps097.shtml (accessed August 3, 2005).

If you now have that distemper, which you have been threatened with, you are separated from your earthly friends, as none of them can come to see you; and if you should die of it, you have taken a final and everlasting leave of them while you are yet alive, so as not to have comfort of their presence and immediate care, and never to see them again in the land of the living. And if you have escaped that distemper, it is by remarkable providence that you are preserved. And your having been so exposed to it, must certainly be a loud call of God, not to trust in earthly friends or anything here below. Young persons are very apt to trust in parents and friends when they think of being on a death-bed. But this providence remarkably teaches you the need of a better Friend and a better Parent, than earthly parents are; one who is every where present, and all-sufficient, that cannot be kept off by infectious distempers, who is able to save from death, or to make happy in death, to save from eternal misery, and to bestow eternal life. It is indeed comfortable, when one is in great pain, and languishing under sore sickness, to have the presence and kind care of near and dear earthly friends; but this is a very small thing, in comparison to what it is, to have the presence of a heavenly Father, and a compassionate and almighty Redeemer.

In God's favor is life, and his loving kindness is better than life. Whether you are in sickness or health, you infinitely need this. But you must know, however great need you stand in of it, you do not deserve it: neither is God the obliged to bestow it upon you, for your standing in need of it, your earnest desiring of it, your crying to him constantly for it from fear of misery, and taking much pains. Till you have savingly believed in Christ, all your desires, and pains, and prayers lay God under no obligation; and if they were ten thousand times as great as they are, you must still know, that you would be in the hands of a sovereign God, who will have mercy on whom he will have mercy.

Indeed, God often hears the poor miserable cries of sinful vile creatures, who have no manner of true regard to Him in their hearts; for he is a God of infinite mercy, and he delights to show mercy for his Son's sake, who is worthy, though you are unworthy, who came to save the sinful and the miserable, yea, some of the chief of sinners. Therefore, there is your only hope: and in him must be your refuge, who invites you to come to him, and says, "Him that come to me I will in no way cast out." Whatever your circumstances are, it is your duty not to despair, but to hope in infinite mercy, through a Redeemer. We are expressly commanded to call upon God in the day of trouble, and when we are afflicted, then to pray. But, if I hear that you have escaped,—either that you have not been sick, or are restored,—though I shall rejoice, and have great cause of thankfulness, yet I shall be concerned for you. If your escape should be followed with carelessness and security, and forgetting the remarkable warning you have had, and God's great mercy in your deliverance, it would be in some respects be more awful than sore sickness.

> It would be very provoking to God, and would probably issue in an increasing hardness of heart; and, it may be, divine vengeance may soon overtake you. I have known various instances of persons being remarkably warned, in providence, by being brought into very dangerous circumstances, and escaping, and afterwards death has soon followed in another way. I earnestly desire, that God would make you wise to salvation, and that he would be merciful and gracious to you in every respect, according as he knows your circumstances require. And this is the daily prayer of
>
> Your affectionate and tender father,
> JONATHAN EDWARDS.[11]

Jonathan Edwards serves as a clear example of how a life of influence cannot only have great impact in its own generation, but by the grace of God can also serve as the foundation for a legacy that can carry on for generation after generation. As a man of integrity and insight, Edwards lived a life worthy of the one who called him. He lived with the intensity of spiritual battle. Edwards led in spiritual awakening and revival. He led in missions and in education. Most of all, Jonathan Edwards led with conviction and purpose, and he led generationally. He always understood that God had entrusted to him the stewardship of His people, and He always led those people from where they were to spiritual maturity, spiritual multiplication and for the glory of God.

---

[11] "Letter to his eldest son," *The Works of Jonathan Edwards, Volume 1,* page clvi, Banner of Truth Trust, Carlisle, Pennsylvania; 1995.

CHAPTER 8

PURPOSE:
Why We Lead

And Jesus came up and spoke to them, saying, "All authority has been given to Me in heaven and on earth. Go therefore and make disciples of all the nations, baptizing them in the name of the Father and the Son and the Holy Spirit, teaching them to observe all that I commanded you; and lo, I am with you always, even to the end of the age." MATTHEW 28:18–20

Indeed, the next generation of great leaders is already evolving, but today's adults may be too preoccupied to notice. Wise churches will explore leadership opportunities for their teenagers rather than waiting until they are adults to begin finding avenues for them to lead.
      Henry Blackaby
      Spiritual Leadership

We are called to be spiritual leaders in whatever sphere of influence we may live. God calls us to be examples of those who believe, to walk in a manner worthy of our calling, and to go and make disciples. It is clear from this calling that God has a purpose for our being here and particularly for our leadership. Therefore, as we lead with integrity, vision, and intensity, we must understand why we lead. More than just being able to say, "because God commands us to," we must be able to move beyond the "Sunday School answer" and know God's purpose in calling us to be examples. While Matthew 28 makes it clear what God's ultimate purpose is, there is within that statement at least three legitimate goals we ought to have for leading spiritually, regardless of whether we are leading at home, church, school, work or play. Those goals are spiritual maturity, spiritual multiplication, and spiritual magnification.

Leading toward Spiritual Maturity

Henry Blackaby, in his book *Spiritual Leadership*, says that it should be the ultimate goal of every spiritual leader to take their people from where they are to where God wants them to be. So much of our church life centers on activity. Therefore, we measure where people are spiritually by their involvement in the activity of the church or their overall spiritual activity. As spiritual leaders, we must fight the temptation to take the easy road. We must discipline ourselves to see the people we lead through spiritual eyes and understand that God's primary concern is for who they are and not what they do. Therefore, our concern should be moving people from where they are to where God wants them to be in their relationship to Him, from spiritual death or infancy to spiritual maturity, not just through some spiritual process or set of activities. We are to go and make disciples.

So, what does it mean to be spiritually mature? First, it should not mean that we have come to look like everyone else in our church. It must not mean that we have jumped through all of the appropriate spiritual hoops to achieve certain status in our church. It is not even defined by reading our Bible, praying, or witnessing to the lost, though I believe those things certainly serve as both a means and a fruit. In my honest study of Scripture, I believe that spiritual maturity is principally made up of three characteristics;

wholeness in Christ, wisdom, and peace with God.

Spiritual maturity is first being made whole in Christ. 1 Corinthians 1:1–3 shows us a picture of believers who lacked spiritual maturity because they were not complete in their relationships with Christ. Their essential problem was that they were trying to add something to their relationship with God to make it more fulfilling and to make themselves feel more significant, more complete.

> *And I, brethren, could not speak to you as to spiritual men, but as to men of flesh, as to infants in Christ. I gave you milk to drink, not solid food; for you were not yet able to receive it. Indeed, even now you are not yet able, for you are still fleshly. For since there is jealousy and strife among you, are you not fleshly, and are you not walking like mere men?*

Paul had given them spiritual milk to drink in their infancy because he recognized that they were not ready to receive the deeper revelation of the things of God. After the passage of considerable time, Paul finds that they are still "not mature" and "fleshly." What is the evidence that they are not mature? Paul says that there is jealousy and strife. Philippians 2:14–16 tells us that we are to do everything without complaining or arguing, so that we may be blameless and pure. Before, we talked about this in terms of the connection between our attitude and our integrity. However, in this context, this verse gives us insight into why Paul finds jealousy and strife to be marks of the spiritually immature.

Jealousy is all about self and is the root of what Paul calls "complaining" in Philippians. When we complain or are jealous, we are driven by pride and thinking more highly of ourselves than we ought. We want what someone else has, or we complain because we do not have what we think we deserve. Because we have not been made complete in Christ, we feel as though we are lacking what we need to have joy in our lives. We feel like we are entitled to something more. Though we put on our mask and play the righteous game, we find that deep within ourselves there are still empty places. No matter how much we hide those places, we still feel the need to fill those voids in our lives. That always reveals itself by jealousy and complaining and shows a deficiency in our relationship with God.

Strife comes from the same root of pride. There are some debates that are extremely valuable for us to have as believers, and there are issues of conviction and faith upon which we should never cease to stand firm. Unfortunately, most of the strife that exists in our churches, youth groups, and families has absolutely nothing to do with spiritual issues of conviction. In fact, most of us cannot list more than one or two issues that would pass as issues of conviction. Most of what we have to argue about are matters of preference or understanding.

In matters of preference or understanding, there is no room for strife. When we argue about such issues, Paul says that it shows a lack of spiritual maturity. In fact, that is exactly what is going on in the Corinthians verse. The people there had decided that some liked Paul more than Apollos. Others, of course, had decided that they would rather follow Paul. Paul himself says that neither Paul nor Apollos was the issue. It was God who had worked in their lives and it was God that should be the focus of all of their admiration and attention. Because we are still immature and proud, we insist on being right. That means that the other person has to be wrong, and we must argue or create strife until we have been declared right before the entire world.

To be spiritually mature is to have the attitude of Christ, as Paul explains in Philippians 3. We are to humble ourselves and empty out ourselves completely so that we can be completely filled with and made complete in Christ. When Christ stood before Pilate and was being judged unjustly, He had every right to make

His case, but He did not argue. He was made complete by His relationship with the Father and refused to be defined by any other. When He hung on that cross, was beaten and scorned, He had every right to complain, but He displayed grace instead. If the Son of God did not complain or argue, why do we? We are so quick to claim our rights and refuse our freedom, to hold to our pride and lose true humility. We can only be spiritually mature when we are free from the flesh and its selfishness and pride.

Spiritual maturity, secondly, is discipline and discernment—wisdom. Paul says to the Corinthians, *"Yet we do speak wisdom among those who are mature; a wisdom, however, not of this age nor of the rulers of this age, who are passing away; but we speak God's wisdom in a mystery, the hidden wisdom which God predestined before the ages for our glory."* Now this is a wisdom that comes only from a dependence on the Spirit of God and, therefore, is the direct result of being spiritually mature.

This wisdom of God is spoken in a divine mystery, and it reveals itself in an ability to discern things spiritually. It requires that we see things through spiritual eyes and judge things not in human terms but in spiritual terms. Wisdom is a discernment that understands our spiritual battle and can know what is from God and what is from the devil. It is a discernment that helps us know when we are under attack and how we should respond. Wisdom is so much more than knowledge, but as Proverbs says, wisdom is the beginning of knowledge, for wisdom is the fear of the Lord.

The wisdom of God is also revealed in self-discipline. Over and over again, we see that self-discipline and wisdom are related. There is probably no better instance of this than in Proverbs 3:7–14.

> *Do not be wise in your own eyes;*
> *Fear the LORD and turn away evil.*
> *It will be healing to your body*

> *And refreshment to your bones.*
> *Honor the LORD from your wealth*
> *And from the first of all your produce;*
> *So your barns will be filled with plenty*
> *And your vats will overflow with new wine.*
> *My son, do not reject the discipline of the LORD*
> *Or loathe His reproof,*
> *For whom the LORD loves He reproves,*
> *Even as a father corrects the son in whom he delights.*
> *How blessed is the man who finds wisdom*
> *And the man who gains understanding.*
> *For her profit is better than the profit of silver*
> *And her gain better than fine gold.*

It is because wisdom is self-disciplined and produces self-discipline that Paul urges Timothy to show wisdom and to be spiritually self-disciplined. *"But have nothing to do with worldly fables fit only for old women. On the other hand, discipline yourself for the purpose of godliness; for bodily discipline is only of little profit, but godliness is profitable for all things, since it holds promise for the present life and also for the life to come."* Discipline yourself to be godly, which is wisdom and spiritual maturity.

I believe that wisdom and spiritual maturity are so closely tied together in Scripture because you cannot have one without the other. I believe one of the marks of spiritual maturity is when the decisions in your life change. Not just that you start to make wise decisions, but that the nature of your decisions change. When we are spiritually babes, we spend a lot of time choosing between good and evil. We are learning how to put off the old and put on the new. As we grow in spiritual maturity, we begin to choose more and more between good and better. This is when we learn to discern what good things might be distracting us from the better things that God has planned for our lives. This is when it is key to not be defined by the opinions and expectations of others.

As our discernment grows and we continue to grow in maturity, we find ourselves most often choosing between better and best. This is when we are living a life of spiritual maturity and we are dependent upon the Holy Spirit to communicate the wisdom of God in our lives. It is often in these times that God seems silent. We have received His wisdom and are maturing. The Father remains quiet while we struggle to discern His best, good, pleasing, and perfect will.

Finally, spiritual maturity is being at peace with God. Peace with God was achieved by Christ on the cross and is applied to us at the moment of our conversion. However, we have to learn to live at peace with God. Though we are no longer enemies of God, our flesh still marches to enemy-like orders. Through discernment and discipline, we come to a place of wholeness and complete unmasked freedom before God. We are made complete in Him; we have nothing about which to argue or complain. It is in this state of living in the wisdom of God that we find ourselves truly humbled and truly unified. I increasingly believe that spiritual maturity is marked more by unity in Christ and submission to Christ than anything else.

It is the mystery of God's will that He will bring everything into unity and submission under the feet, or authority, of Christ in the end. We have already seen that the mystery of the will of God is revealed only to the wise and spiritually mature. It is to those who are mature that God leaves the responsibility of living out His purpose, and that purpose centers on the unity of the body of Christ. I believe that God desires to do a great work in our generation and what He requires to do that work is that His body be unified.

Now we often think of unity of the body in terms of breaking down denominational walls, and this is certainly a huge issue in the modern church. However, I think we would all agree that God does not view us in terms of our denomination as much as in terms of our relationships. Unity in the body is not a denominational issue alone. It is a community issue, a congregational issue, and an individual issue.

Unity is a community issue. In all my years of ministry, I think one of the most discouraging things is how little churches are given to any community work together. It is almost impossible to get local churches to put aside differences, most of them differences of pride and preference, in order to cooperate for the sake of the gospel. The truth is churches are much more competitive and proud than they are unified. It is the source of one of my main "soapboxes" in life. That is, the modern church is more about self-promotion and self-protection than they are about service and sacrifice. This was not the case with the early church. We all live in the same community yet we are too worried about holding onto what we have, arguing, complaining and being jealous of each other, to come together as one body, sacrificially, to serve those in need in our community.

Unity is a congregational issue. There is no greater battlefield in contemporary religious life than inside the walls of the average church. As sad as it is, there is no limit to the territorialism, jealousy, pride and selfishness in the average church. Pastors and elders hold power, committees and departments rival each other for finances and attention, and individuals compete for status and recognition. We look for little things to complain or argue about so that we will be heard and maybe even declared right. We are jealous of status or position, and so we tell tales and scoff. We selfishly hoard our power by oppressing the liberty of others. All the while, we sacrifice only our influence—nothing but our own integrity and spiritual maturity.

Unity is an individual issue. Well, what is left? We do not love our neighbors as ourselves, and the world certainly does not know us for our great love for one another. We spread rumor more than we pray. We are jealous more than we serve. We store up more than we sacrifice. We are more proud than humble and tear down in order to build ourselves up. We hide our true selves out of fear of our brother, and as a result we deny everyone true wholeness and freedom. We build false walls between the young and the old, between the rich and the poor, between the majority and the minority. We all try to look alike and call it unity, but in reality there is no unity apart from individual wholeness, and there is no wholeness without spiritual maturity.

Maturity means to be fully ripe or grown. Thus, to be mature spiritually is to be ripe in the Spirit, to be whole and complete. It means to be fully grown spiritually. To be grown up in the Spirit implies that the Spirit is alive and active in our lives, instructing us in the things of God, in wisdom. The spiritual man is one who walks by the Spirit in the sense of Galatians 5:16–25.

> *But I say, walk by the Spirit, and you will not carry out the desire of the flesh. For the flesh sets its desire against the Spirit, and the Spirit against the flesh; for these are in opposition to one another, so that you may not do the things that you please. But if you are led by the Spirit, you are not under the Law. Now the deeds of the flesh are evident, which are: immorality, impurity, sensuality, idolatry, sorcery, enmities, strife, jealousy, outbursts of anger, disputes, dissensions, factions, envying, drunkenness, carousing, and things like these, of which I forewarn you, just as I have forewarned you, that those who practice such things will not inherit the kingdom of God.*

> *But the fruit of the Spirit is love, joy, peace, patience, kindness, goodness, faithfulness, gentleness, self-control; against such things there is no law. Now those who*

> *belong to Christ Jesus have crucified the flesh with its passions and desires. If we live by the Spirit, let us also walk by the Spirit.*

Who himself manifests the fruit of the Spirit in his own way and who preserves the unity of the Spirit in the bond of peace in the sense of Ephesians 4:1–16. This is what we should strive to be as leaders and what we should be leading towards as spiritual leaders.

> *Therefore I, the prisoner of the Lord, implore you to walk in a manner worthy of the calling with which you have been called, with all humility and gentleness, with patience, showing tolerance for one another in love, being diligent to preserve the unity of the Spirit in the bond of peace. There is one body and one Spirit, just as also you were called in one hope of your calling; one Lord, one faith, one baptism, one God and Father of all who is over all and through all and in all. But to each one of us grace was given according to the measure of Christ's gift.*

> *Therefore it says,*
> *"WHEN HE ASCENDED ON HIGH,*
> *HE LED CAPTIVE A HOST OF CAPTIVES,*
> *AND HE GAVE GIFTS TO MEN."*

> *(Now this expression, "He ascended," what does it mean except that He also had descended into the lower parts of the earth? He who descended is Himself also He who ascended far above all the heavens, so that He might fill all things.)*

And He gave some as apostles, and some as prophets, and some as evangelists, and some as pastors and teachers, for the equipping of the saints for the work of service, to the building up of the body of Christ; until we all attain to the unity of the faith, and of the knowledge of the Son of God, to a mature man, to the measure of the stature which belongs to the fullness of Christ. As a result, we are no longer to be children, tossed here and there by waves and carried about by every wind of doctrine, by the trickery of men, by craftiness in deceitful scheming; but speaking the truth in love, we are to grow up in all aspects into Him who is the head, even Christ, from whom the whole body, being fitted and held together by what every joint supplies, according to the proper working of each individual part, causes the growth of the body for the building up of itself in love.

Leading toward Spiritual Multiplication

Leaders lead followers. Great leaders lead leaders, and a failure to develop leaders is a failure by the leader, whether by design or neglect. It is one of the most common failures of leaders, that we spend too little time or effort preparing our people for our departure. It is an ego thing; none of us want to think about what happens after we are gone, and we certainly don't want to think about how things might go on without us and possibly be better than when we were here.

However, one great test of leadership is how well a leader's legacy continues after they leave. Unless we are intentional about developing leaders, it will not happen. This is evident in the well-documented drop-out rates among Christian teens. Some seventy percent of students who grew up active in a student ministry in the

United States over the past ten years have left the church without any real indication that they intend to return. These are our church kids, our core group. If we are not raising leaders for the next generation in our churches and in our Christian homes, then we are not going to leave a lasting spiritual legacy. Therefore, we are not fulfilling our role as spiritual leaders.

One way that I try to be intentional about developing leaders is through personal discipleship. My primary role as a discipler is to be the primary spiritual influence in the lives of my children. My wife and I, with the help of our church, make an annual plan for the spiritual development of our children. We work to implement that plan each year and expand it as they grow and mature. The main focus is to prepare them to be spiritual leaders even when I am not around.

I also work to maintain what is called a Barnabas, Paul, Timothy model of spiritual multiplication. The idea is to have a more mature believer who is mentoring me and speaking into my life spiritually. I like to have two or three of these because I need a lot of work. We do not always meet in a formal discipleship format, but these older men simply pour into me what they have been receiving from God in their own lives, and holding me accountable. In turn, I try to keep about three younger believers into whose life I am speaking. I try to disciple and mentor them. Some are more formal than others, but I mostly try to give them resources and pour into them what God has been pouring into me. That is why I see my life as investing in the lives of those who invest in the lives of others. It is because I believe so strongly in this spiritual multiplication process.

There are at least four practices leaders must adopt to produce a core of leaders around them—disciples who make disciples: delegation, giving freedom to fail, recognize success, encourage and support.

The first practice a leader must adopt is the practice of delegation. When I talk to volunteers about their role on a ministry team, I always talk to them about the difficulty of delegation. For a leader to delegate authority and responsibility is very difficult because he or she is the leader. It is hard to give your authority over in an area or event to someone and make them responsible for it when you understand that their passion, commitment, dedication and expertise are all less then your own and no matter how much they are responsible to you and the team for the area, you are ultimately responsible before God. It would be much easier to delegate if the people we lead understood the difficulty of delegation. However, leaders must learn to delegate if they are going to be successful and if they are going to leave a lasting legacy of leadership.

There are some things that you are not good at. It is hard to admit sometimes, but it is true of all of us. We serve our people better when we learn to hand over the things that we cannot do. There are also some things that we can do but that we are not particularly called to do and are therefore not a top priority for us to do. We make ourselves much more efficient if we hand over things that we can do, but that others can do just as well. There are things that others do better than us. This is the hardest thing for us to hand over. This is something that we do well, but someone else around us or on our team may do it better. That is hard to admit as a leader sometimes, but we make our team better when everyone is doing what they do best. When 20% of the people do 80% of the work in church, we rob people of an opportunity to serve, and we end up doing things poorly, fairly, or well that someone else could be great at doing. We have to hand these things over and focus on what only we as leaders should do, can do and what we do best. This not only makes us better but gives others an opportunity to serve, learn, and grow.

The main thing in delegation is never to abdicate or give over a role or responsibility to someone else that God has given particularly to you. We all have different gifts and abilities, and we all have different roles as a result. However, we must be mindful never to delegate a biblical role or responsibility. As parents, children, teachers, students and preachers, we must work to know and understand our unique roles and those of the people around us so that we can protect those roles and encourage others in them.

If we adopt the practice of delegation, the next practice we must adopt is giving freedom to fail. When we hand over these valuable areas to others who may do as well or better than us, we also have to realize that they have to learn, grow and develop into those roles. Nobody wants to fail, but in order to learn and grow we have to have the freedom to fail. A gymnast does not go out and do an Olympic floor routine her first time on the mat. I guarantee that every one fell their first time. I cannot imagine what happens on those parallel bars!

The best example of this that I have ever experienced is when we had to start a student worship ministry from scratch. We started with one guy who could sing choruses and play three chords on a guitar. He was nervous and hard to follow at first, but it was not that bad. Soon, he invited a friend to play guitar along with him. Things got a little better, but they were still not leading worship. Over the next few months, they were joined by a few other musicians and began to practice together. It got worse for a while as they learned to play together, but as they learned, matured and grew they began to come together musically. After a two-year journey, they became a fairly accomplished group and were one of the main draws for our ministry.

The point is, I could have tried to lead worship myself or recruited adult volunteers to lead worship. We could have even hired someone to come in and lead worship for us until we formed a group. Any of those options would have been better than what we had in the beginning, though none of those options would have produced the long-term result of developing student leaders. It would have been easier to delegate to adults than to students, but they never would have been such a vital part of our ministry. We had to give it to them and give them room to stink for a while in order to have the best student-led worship services around.

This is true for us as leaders as well. When I talk to parents about the concept of family worship, one of the common responses is that they do not feel equipped to lead their family in worship. First, that is a failure of the church leadership that we have not equipped parents to do what God has uniquely called them to do. Second, you cannot fail in leading your family in worship. You have to give yourself permission to try and come up short. You have to be willing to start, and if you do not maintain it, start again. Start small and simple. We started with three mornings a week, just singing "Jesus Loves Me," reading a story from a children's Bible and saying a prayer together.

When you begin to delegate and give room for growth, you soon learn how key it is to recognize the success of others. One of the most important things we can do as leaders is to shine the light of praise on those around us. If we are going to establish a high standard by which to live and hold each other accountable, we have to be just as quick to recognize the success and accomplishments of others. This is one of the most important lessons I ever learned as a student minister. I expected a lot out of my students and volunteers. When I learned that they needed me to recognize their contributions and achievements and I did so, they began to contribute and achieve more. Two things I always tried to do were to recognize them personally and recognize them publicly.

When the people we lead do what is expected of them or live up to the standard placed before them, I believe we ought to recognize them privately and let them know that you notice a job well done. When they perform at that level over time or they exceed expectation or make an outstanding contribution, we should find a way to recognize them publicly. Find a way. Send a card or make a phone call. Buy a lunch or give a prize. Bring your leaders up in front of the people and recognize them in front of their peers. If we are going to ask them to do this and that and to not do this and that, we must recognize them when they meet those standards. Never forget to pay attention to the little things over time. Anyone can jump through a hoop; those who perform over time are your real leaders.

A leader also recognizes that not all the people we lead will be successful all of the time, and even the most successful will struggle. That is why we not only recognize achievement, but we also encourage and support. First, we are to encourage. This literally means to give courage to. When the people we serve are down, struggling or defeated, it is our job to show grace. When we give grace to our people, we give them courage, and when people are encouraged, they have hope. Giving hope to the people we lead is what our calling is all about. We give hope that they can succeed and become what God created and called them to be.

Second, we are to support. To support means to hold up. I know this may be a foreign concept to many of us in the church, but it is our biblical responsibility to lift each other up, to bear one another's burdens. When the people we serve fall, we are to lift. When they stumble, we catch. When they grow weary, we hold them up. You know, when Jesus went to the cross, God gave a great example of our role when Jesus' cross was handed over to Simon the Cyrene. We have to hold our people up and support them mentally, physically, emotionally and spiritually. We do not lead because of where people can carry us. We lead because of where we can help carry people. That is a ministry of service and sacrifice.

Leading toward Spiritual Magnification

It does not matter in what sphere of life we are leading, our goal ought to be to glorify God in the way we lead and to lead others to glorify God. God is not concerned with bringing glory to people, but in revealing His glory through people. None of us do this naturally. Our natural instinct is to bring glory to ourselves, and we have to fight pretty hard not to rob God of His glory. If we think our homes and churches naturally glorify God, we are wrong. As we lead, we have to lead people to die to themselves and take up their cross daily. We have to remind them that it is us who belong on that cross and Jesus who belongs on the throne of our lives. Colossians 3 gives us some good insight into how we should approach leading for the glory of God and leading others to glorify God.

The first insight is found in verse 2, which says, *"Set your mind on the things above, not on the things that are on earth."* This may sound like a simple idea at first. However, it seems to be at the heart of our struggle as leaders. We have to work to have divine insight because we are bound by the perspective of this world unless we are set free by God. Once we are set free and gain a divine perspective on life and this world, we still struggle to lead according to the things above. It is easy to allow the circumstances of this world to direct our path. It is equally difficult to get the people we lead to look beyond the temporal and the immediate into the eternal. That is why vision is so important. It is so much more than giving people a picture of what God has for their future. It is teaching them to set their minds on the things above. As leaders who want to leave a lasting legacy, we must understand that our first calling is not to be successful in the world, but to be a success in the Kingdom of God. And our legacy will be how successful those who follow us are in their dependence and obedience to God.

The second insight is found in verses 23–24. *"Whatever you do, do your work heartily, as for the Lord rather than for men, knowing that from the Lord you will receive the reward of the inheritance, it is the Lord Christ whom you serve."* We also have to understand that no matter what our role is and what we may be doing, we are to do it as though we are in the direct service of the Lord, because we are! Service and sacrifice are the two marks of any true disciple. As leaders, we have to help our people understand that we cannot compartmentalize our lives and create areas that are not sacrificed to God. Where there is no sacrifice, there can be no true service. If there is any area of life where we are not serving God, it is an area that is a waste of our time. Everything we do should be part of offering our bodies as living sacrifices to God, because this is our service to God. We have to understand that we serve God with all of our lives; our recreational life, home life, work life, school life, as well as our religious life.

CHAPTER 9
MOSES:
A Legacy Leadership Model

"So now, go. I am sending you to Pharaoh to bring my people the Israelites out of Egypt." But Moses said to God, "Who am I that I should go to Pharaoh and bring the Israelites out of Egypt?" And God said, "I will be with you. And this will be the sign to you that it is I who have sent you: When you have brought the people out of Egypt, you will worship God on this mountain." Moses said to God, "Suppose I go to the Israelites and say to them, 'The God of your fathers has sent me to you,' and they ask me, 'What is his name?' Then what shall I tell them?" God said to Moses, "I am who I am. This is what you are to say to the Israelites: 'I AM has sent me to you.'" God also said to Moses, "Say to the Israelites, 'The LORD, the God of your fathers—the God of Abraham, the God of Isaac and the God of Jacob—has sent me to you.' This is my name forever, the name by which I am to be remembered from generation to generation." EXODUS 3:10–15

God's greatest gifts to Israel, better than the land itself, were men such as Moses and David and Isaiah. God's greatest gifts are always men; His greatest endowment to the church was the gift of twelve men trained for leadership.

J. Oswald Sanders
Spiritual Leadership

We are all familiar with the epic narrative of the life of Moses that runs throughout four books of the Old Testament, from Exodus through Deuteronomy. His story is one that is rich with wisdom and adventure. However, as a leader, there is no one who parallels Moses. From the most humble of beginnings, God brought Moses to a place where he was the most influential person in the Old Testament.

There is so much more of value in Moses' life than we could ever hope to cover in this one chapter. However, we can look at the life of Moses simply as a model of the kind of legacy leadership that we have been discussing in this book. The best way to accomplish this task is to look at Moses' life along three natural breaks, which loosely represent the stages of influence, impact, and legacy as we have laid them out here. Moses was 120 years old when he died on Mount Nebo, and his life can be measured by three forty-year segments.

The House of Pharaoh: Standard and Influence

The story opens in Egypt, where Jacob and his family had settled and lived for four hundred years. In the thirteenth century BCE, a new Pharaoh came to power in Egypt who was a great builder, but who had no respect for the Hebrew people. In order to build his great cities, he made the Hebrew people slaves and put them to work in forced labor camps. He feared they would revolt against him because they became great in number, so he ordered that every male infant be killed at birth.

Moses was born to Amram and Jochebed, who were from the line of priests called Levites. We know how Moses was saved by being hidden for three months and then being floated down the river in a basket. Pharaoh's daughter found Moses and had him fished out of the river. She felt sorry for him and decided to keep him. So, Moses grew up as the adopted son of the Pharaoh.

However, Moses was always aware of his true heritage as a Hebrew because God made a way for his mother to be his nurse and to raise him in the house of Pharaoh. This is all-important to us because this is the context in which God established a standard of excellence in Moses' life and gave him influence.

Moses spent the first forty years of his life living in one of the great societies of human history. Living in the house of Pharaoh, he was trained in language, art, law, engineering, and all of the sciences of his day. Having been raised by his Levite mother, he was instructed in the heritage of the Hebrew people and nurtured in a love for the God of Abraham, Isaac, and Jacob.

Moses was being given the foundational preparation that He would need to become who God had created and called him to be. However, though he had a position of influence as a member of the house of Pharaoh and was a person of influence among his own people, he was not yet ready to have the impact that God intended for him to have. In fact, in Exodus 2:11-12, we read how Moses tried to use his position to take matters into his own hands. *"Now it came about in those days, when Moses had grown up, that he went out to his brethren and looked on their hard labors; and he saw an Egyptian beating a Hebrew, one of his brethren. So he looked this way and that, and when he saw there was no one around, he struck down the Egyptian and hid him in the sand."*

In the very next verse, we see that Moses again tried to use his persona to take matters into his own hands. *"He went out the next day, and behold, two Hebrews were fighting with each other; and he said to the offender, 'Why are you striking your companion?'"* Though Moses had been raised to live up to a standard that called him to defend and lead his people, he did not yet have the integrity and insight to do so. Though he had been given a position of authority, the rest of the passage reveals that his lack of integrity and vision had caused him to not walk in a manner worthy of his calling. *"But he said, 'Who made you a prince or a judge over us? Are you intending to kill me as you killed the Egyptian?' Then Moses was afraid and said, 'Surely the matter has become known.' When Pharaoh heard of this matter, he tried to kill Moses. But Moses fled from the presence of Pharaoh and settled in the land of Midian, and he sat down by a well."*

Despite the advantages of what God had done in his life to this point, Moses lacked integrity, vision and a godly life. This did not produce a life of impact and legacy, but one of fear, fleeing, and loneliness.

The House of Jethro: Integrity, Insight, Imitation, Intensity

As Moses sat there by that well, he had no idea of what God had in store for him. He must have thought his life was ruined, finished, over. Yet God was getting ready to take him from the house of Pharaoh to the house of Jethro, from the house of a king, to the house of a priest. In the house of the priest of Midian, Moses would find wholeness, a picture of what God had planned for his future, and his feet on holy ground.

It is no accident that whenever God is getting ready to do something extraordinary in the life of someone, they often have to go through a time of great trial and often "hit bottom." There is no saying why this is for sure. I suspect it has something to do with humility and understanding grace, and the fact that God chooses the least things of this world to make the greatest in the Kingdom. I am sure if we asked Abraham, David, Peter, Paul, or Moses for that matter, they would tell us about coming to understand our dependence on God and that it has to do with God getting all of the glory for what He is about to do. Whatever God's purpose for doing it, He most often does, and this is where Moses finds himself.

Here is our hero, Moses, feeling scared, alone, tired, and desperate. But God was not through with him yet. In fact, he was right where God wanted him. As Moses sat there by that well, the seven daughters of Jethro, the priest of a nomadic Midian tribe, came to water their flocks. Like any desperate man, he helped the ladies out, fighting off shepherds who tried to run them off and then drawing water for them. Is this a great story or what? The daughters went home and told their father about the stranger at the well and he sent for Moses to come and eat with them. I love the Bible right here. *"Moses was willing to dwell with the man, and he gave his daughter Zipporah to Moses. Then she gave birth to a son, and he named him Gershom, for he said, 'I have been a sojourner in a foreign land.'"*

Let's not call it a comeback yet, but God has a way of putting us in a better place. Jethro was a wise man, and in his house Moses learned contentment. Moses would spend the next forty years tending the sheep of Jethro. During this time, he grew close to God. He learned to have integrity and found wholeness in his life. Moses matured as he fought off the wild beast and protected the sheep in the desert. He found a context for his life and most importantly, he found his heart in his wife Zipporah and his two sons.

Meanwhile, the Israelites were crying out because of their suffering, and the king who had made them slaves died. God heard them and purposed to keep the covenant He had made with Abraham, Isaac, and Jacob to make them a great nation and give them a land of their own. As Moses was becoming what God created and called him to be, God was developing a picture of his future for him to see. It was time for Moses to learn insight.

We all know that while Moses was tending sheep near Mount Horeb, the mountain of God, he saw a bush burning but not being consumed. The Bible says that the angel of the Lord appeared to him in a flame of fire from the midst of a bush. Moses saw unbelievable circumstances but he did not yet see God. He lacked vision, divine perspective, purpose, and plan. Seeing this, God called to him.

> *"Moses, Moses!" And he said, "Here I am." Then He said, "Do not come near here; remove your sandals from your feet, for the place on which you are standing is holy ground." He said also, "I am the God of your father, the God of Abraham, the God of Isaac, and the God of Jacob." Then Moses hid his face, for he was afraid to look at God.* EXODUS 3:4-6

Moses was about to get a clear picture of what God had planned for his future.

> *The LORD said, "I have surely seen the affliction of My people who are in Egypt, and have given heed to their cry because of their taskmasters, for I am aware of their sufferings. So I have come down to deliver them from the power of the Egyptians, and to bring them up from that land to a good and spacious land, to a land flowing with milk and honey, to the place of the Canaanite and the Hittite and the Amorite and the Perizzite and the Hivite and the Jebusite. Now, behold, the cry of the sons of Israel has come to Me; furthermore, I have seen the oppression with which the Egyptians are oppressing them. Therefore, come now, and I will send you to Pharaoh, so that you may bring My people, the sons of Israel, out of Egypt."* EXODUS 3:7-10

There is a lot to learn here about vision and how it works. First, God saw the need of His people. It did not matter that forty years before Moses had seen the need of his people. It is all about what God's perspective and timing. They are keys to fulfilling God's plan for your life. When Moses tried to take matters into his own hands, things did not turn out so well.

Second, God makes it clear that He has come to deliver His

people from the power of the Egyptians. He is not calling Moses to set them free. We have to be careful to not take on God's role in fulfilling His plan. God came to deliver Israel and bring them to the Promised Land. God says, "I have heard my people and I will bring them out into a good and spacious land. Now you come and go to Pharaoh so that you can lead them out." Our role as spiritual leaders is not to do God's work of moving His people, but to lead them from where they are to where He wants them to be.

I do not believe that Moses responded with false humility or lack of faith. I believe he simply remembered vividly the circumstances that caused him to leave Egypt. When Moses sincerely asked God, "Who am I?" it is in this wonderful moment that Moses learns the value of imitation. God says, "It does not matter who you are, I am with you." I love how God goes back to the vision to confirm for Moses that He will be with him. "*But I will be with you, and this shall be the sign for you, that I have sent you: when you have brought the people out of Egypt, you shall serve God on this mountain.*" You will know that I am with you because when you are done doing what I have called you to do, you will worship Me right here!

Moses rightly understands that he did not have influence with his people any longer because he lacked integrity before them in the past. He asked a legitimate question, "Under what authority do I tell them I come? In whose name do I go, for I cannot go in my own name?"

> *God said to Moses, "I AM WHO I AM." And he said, "Say this to the people of Israel, 'I AM has sent me to you.'" God also said to Moses, "Say this to the people of Israel, 'The LORD, the God of your fathers, the God of Abraham, the God of Isaac, and the God of Jacob, has sent me to you.' This is my name forever, and thus I am to be remembered throughout all generations."* EXODUS 3:14–15

Only through imitation does Moses have credibility with the people to lead them from where they are to where God wants them to be. It was not Moses, but God with Moses. Moses will not say, "Let my people go". The Lord will say it. It is in the name of God and by His authority that Moses will do battle with Pharaoh. Now God speaks with the intensity of that battle, giving Moses a sense of urgency about what God has called him to do.

> *Go and gather the elders of Israel together and say to them, "The LORD, the God of your fathers, the God of Abraham, of Isaac, and of Jacob, has appeared to me, saying, 'I have observed you and what has been done to you in Egypt, and I promise that I will bring you up out of the affliction of Egypt to the land of the Canaanites, the Hittites, the Amorites, the Perizzites, the Hivites, and the Jebusites, a land flowing with milk and honey.'" And they will listen to your voice, and you and the elders of Israel shall go to the king of Egypt and say to him, 'The LORD, the God of the Hebrews, has met with us; and now, please let us go a three days' journey into the wilderness, that we may sacrifice to the LORD our God." But I know that the king of Egypt will not let you go unless compelled by a mighty hand. So I will stretch out my hand and strike Egypt with all the wonders that I will do in it; after that he will let you go.* EXODUS 3:16–20

Here we see God give Moses those three essential elements of intensity. First, God empowers Moses and the children of Israel for the battle by giving them an assurance that He has seen their suffering and that He will act accordingly. God rightly evaluates the current reality, giving them the power of the intensity of their circumstances.

Second, God prepares the people for what He is about to do by giving them a promise for the future. God knew the people would need to be encouraged in order to persevere through the battle. So, He gives them a clear picture of what He has planned for their future in order to prepare them for battle.

Finally, God gives them a plan of attack. He tells them not only what He is going to do for them, but exactly how He is going to use them to do it. "This is what you will do, this is what he will do, then, this is what I will do and this is what will happen! I will work all things for good to those who love me and are called according to My purpose."

The Children of God: Leading to Maturity, Multiplication, and Glory

Moses spent the last third of his life fulfilling God's purpose. In what we would consider his retirement years, Moses led the nation of Israel out of Egypt, through the desert, to the Promised Land. During that time, God used him to deliver His law, to appoint judges over the nation, to purify the nation and to appoint the next generation leader. During this time, we see Moses use all that God had taught him throughout his life to lead his people in a way that would lead them to maturity, lead them to lead themselves, and lead them to glorify God. There are several principles that become obvious during this phase in Moses' life that we can apply in helping us become Legacy Leaders.

The first principle that we see displayed during this period of Moses' life is God-centeredness. That is what Christ as the standard in our lives is all about. God empowers us to lead when He calls us to lead. We do not have to be the best speakers, we do not have to have a position or title, and we do not even have to be perfect people. We just have to depend on the grace of God and the strength of His might. We have to wait patiently for Him and not move out before He sends us. We must also be so ready to move that when He calls our name we are instant. Again, Blackaby says in his book *Spiritual Leadership*, "He (God) ask leaders to walk with Him so intimately that, when He reveals what is on His agenda, they will immediately adjust their lives to His will and the results will bring glory to God." Legacy is not about me, but God doing great things through me. God told Moses, "I will be with you." At every step of the journey, God gave Moses supernatural influence because Moses was completely dependant on God. Because Moses had established God as the center of his life, Israel heard him when He spoke in God's name, Pharaoh heard him when he acted in God's name, and the Red Sea even heard him when he moved in God's name.

Second, we see the principle of influence displayed in the life of Moses. We have already seen how God gave Moses supernatural influence because He was centered on God. However, we also see Moses use that influence to challenge Israel's old way of life. To lead implies a new direction. The people of God could not stay tethered to Egypt. They could not become free men and women without making the journey through the wilderness. Only then would they have the souls of free men and dwell in the Promised Land. Leaders must challenge the old and anticipate resistance. The journey would not be easy. There would be plagues and elemental barriers. There would be Pharaoh's army and a desert. There would be idols and giants. However, through the leadership of Moses, God would provide gold and miracles, victory and manna, a covenant and a Promised Land.

Third, we see the principle of integrity. Leadership holds people and organizations accountable to the godly standard. Moses ascended to receive the law, and the people quickly forgot the vision and regressed to their old way, corrupting themselves. When God became angry and was set to destroy the people, Moses took responsibility for the people he was leading. Then, Moses went to the people and held God's truth up before their delusion. He showed the people that they must be faithful to the one true God. Moses was responsible to impose fidelity to the original. When the people revert back and corrupt themselves, the leader must intercede, destroy the graven idols and refocus the people on the purpose of the journey—the Promised Land. As a result, God made a covenant with His people.

The fourth essential element we see displayed in the life of Moses is vision. The Hebrews prayed for liberation for hundreds of years, but it was not until God decided to initiate it that the change became a reality. Moses questioned his selection by God as a change agent, his ability to confront the old establishment and his credibility to lead the people—just like all of us do. However, God revealed to Moses what He had purposed to do. The vision, "the land of milk and honey," is the responsibility of the leadership. God showed Moses the vision, and it was up to Moses to keep the vision ever in front of the people. When they were afraid, he had to remind them of the vision. When they were tired, he had to remind them of the vision. When they fell into sin, Moses had to keep the picture God had planned for their future in front of them. By staff, by pillar of fire, by stone tablet, or by temple tent, Moses kept the picture of what God had promised in plain view.

Fifth, we see the principle of imitation, as Moses demonstrates an attitude of hope, built on the promises of God. Even after many years, when they've almost achieved their vision, the children of Israel still did not have the heart of free people. The Lord told Moses to send in spies to the Promised Land. When they returned, ten among the leaders of the children of Israel had lost the vision and gave a fearful report. The people of God murmured. Spiritual leadership is always optimistic. Only Joshua and Caleb were optimist. Upon hearing the negative reports of the others, they tore their clothes. The congregation begged to stone them with stones, but God protected them. Of the founding fathers, only Joshua and

Caleb ever entered the Promised Land. While the murmuring of the people kept them wandering in the wilderness and their lack of faith in God kept all but the two optimists from seeing the vision with their eyes, the future leaders of the nation were not deterred by giants and were able to savor the reality of the vision in the Promised Land.

Leaders often must challenge the realistic, or pessimistic, majority and offer an unpopular divine perspective. It took forty years for the old generation to die. It took forty years for the next generation to develop, a courageous generation with holy and free souls, men and women who honored God. Then, they were a nation of people who imitated the nature and character of God.

The sixth characteristic of Legacy Leadership we see in the life of Moses is intensity. The people of God cried out to the Lord, and cried out to Moses saying, "We should have stayed in Egypt!" In the heat of battle, the people crumbled under the intensity. They were not always equipped to deal with where God was leading them, but God's chosen leader was. Moses quieted the people, admonished them to have faith and told them the Lord would lead the way. The Lord empowered Moses to part the waters. The children of Israel did not want to let go of the old. Although they wanted to be free, it was too difficult to let go. At the first sign of difficulty, Israel began to complain—better to die in the old familiar world than in pressing on to take hold of a future hope. Of course they took the knowledge of the old with them, and reverted back to it as soon as Moses was out of sight, so Moses had to destroy the old completely.

The people of Israel so lacked an understanding of intensity, that they were willing to be slaves for a few onions and a pepper. Moses understood what was at stake and that God had burned the old bridges back to insure that the people of God would not step in the same river twice. Unless those Hebrews could walk on water, they would not return to the old. They had been led through a parted sea, and they would either receive the promise of God or die in the wilderness.

Seventh, Moses displayed maturity. He had learned the idea of wholeness. What he learned about himself and about life while tending the sheep gave him a unity of purpose in his spirit. He was a strong leader and exercised judgment over the people with great wisdom. Most of all, we see that in the end, Moses was at peace with God.

Moses also displays for us multiplication, though, like most of us, he needed a little help with this one. Moses overburdened himself with the demands of leadership, and had to be instructed to empower those around him. In Exodus 18:13–26, we see a perfect picture of why spiritual leadership is to always be engaged in delegating out both authority and responsibility to the leaders we lead.

> *The next day Moses took his seat to serve as judge for the people, and they stood around him from morning till evening. When his father-in-law saw all that Moses was doing for the people, he said, "What is this you are doing for the people? Why do you alone sit as judge, while all these people stand around you from morning till evening?"*
>
> *Moses answered him, "Because the people come to me to seek God's will. Whenever they have a dispute, it is brought to me, and I decide between the parties and inform them of God's decrees and laws."*

Moses had become overwhelmed by the task of serving the people, and he needed someone else to help him see that it was not good for him or the people. His father-in-law helped him see that just because it needed to be done and he could do it, did not mean that he had to or should do it by himself. Listen to the wisdom of delegation:

> *Moses' father-in-law replied, "What you are doing is not good. You and these people who come to you will only wear yourselves out. The work is too heavy for you; you cannot handle it alone. Listen now to me and I will give you some advice, and may God be with you. You must be the people's representative before God and bring their disputes to him. Teach them the decrees and laws, and show them the way to live and the duties they are to perform. But select capable men from all the people—men who fear God, trustworthy men who hate dishonest gain—and appoint them as officials over thousands, hundreds, fifties and tens. Have them serve as judges for the people at all times, but have them bring every difficult case to you; the simple cases they can decide themselves. That will make your load lighter, because they will share it with you. If you do this and God so commands, you will be able to stand the strain, and all these people will go home satisfied."*

You do what God has called you to do, what only you can do, and you appoint others to handle the rest. Make them accountable to you, give them both authority and responsibility, and then set them free to serve God and grow in their maturity.

> *Moses listened to his father-in-law and did everything he said. He chose capable men from all Israel and made them leaders of the people, officials over thousands, hundreds, fifties and tens. They served as judges for the people at all times. The difficult cases they brought to Moses, but the simple ones they decided themselves.*

Again, Moses not only shows the value of multiplication, but also the fruit of maturity and wisdom. He shows us a humble and teachable spirit, respect of his father-in-law, and trust in God. In Numbers 11, God orders Moses to appoint elders over the people because Moses could no longer bear the burden of leadership alone. A true leader is more a teacher than a judge. The leader must select those he empowers carefully, but leaders must exist at every level. For Moses, they existed over thousands, over hundreds, over fifties, and over tens.

Finally, Moses shows us spiritual magnification. We see this in his understanding that it was never about him. Moses knew he would not live to enter the Promised Land and asked God for his replacement. Good leadership recognizes the importance of constancy of leadership and bridges his leadership with an effective succession strategy, finding a successor early and passing the mantle over time in the sight of the followers. It is often the new leader, anointed in the wilderness, who leads the people into the new vision.

Change is never easy! Transformational change is the most difficult, and great change requires great leadership. However, the glory of God for generation after generation is a great legacy to leave. As spiritual leaders, we have a unique opportunity to provide some necessary and valuable gifts for the next generation. We are at a sacred moment for transformation—urgency. God desires to do a great and mighty work in the next generation. We must provide great leadership.

Moses mentored Joshua and worked to prepare him to lead the nation into the Promised Land. He understood the folly of leaving our work to untrained hands. Moses understood that the journey was never the purpose, nor was his great leadership. The purpose was moving God's people from where they were to where He wanted them to be. The purpose of God was to move Israel from slavery to freedom, from oppression to promise, from Egypt to the Promised Land.

If our lives are to be about God's purposes and the glory of God displayed for generations to come, we must use our influence to challenge the old, impact our people by providing guidance through the process, and leave a legacy of people in our place who are better than us, born in the wilderness, who will enter the Promised Land and be leaders for the next generation.